Praise for Heal Your Soul History

"An inspirational guide to using a soul's long history to combat present-day negative forces."

Kirkus Reviews

"Heal Your Soul History will resonate with those interested in a life of peace and wholeness. Passion over the subject matter is evident throughout. The resultant tone is empowering and conversational. Some notions are striking, particularly fresh ideas about the worth of tears, the potential power of negative thinking, and the process of depression. The inclusion of topics such as bigotry and cultural isolation is also refreshing..."

Margaret Fedder
Foreword Reviews

"...The book is a guide for both, the believers and non-believers of reincarnation, as Dunblazier discusses spirituality extensively and how each unique soul endures it differently. The book is worded in a straightforward style and has easy-to-understand explanations...The book is for everyone who is trying to find a new perspective on the mysteries of life, and particularly for people who find human nature fascinating. FIVE STARS!"

SeriousReading.com

"Excellent book on trying to understand the workings of the soul. Would highly recommend to anyone undertaking the spiritual journey."

Mrs. H Hornsby

"This book is a wonderful resource for healing. I finished it in one day, but I know that the things I learned will stick with me for years to come."

MC

"A highly entertaining and thought provoking read! Anyone interested or curious about past lives should definitely pick up this book. Dunblazier crafted a deeply personal account of her and others' spiritual experiences. She also talks a lot about self-acceptance, love, and healing. Her words are very moving and will give any reader pause for self-reflection."

Anna
Good Reads Review

"The book is filled with dramatic case histories, and Tracee time and again demonstrates her familiarity with a vast number of spiritual practices and techniques. Written in a style that is personable and easy to read, we think that any reader who is in need of assistance of slaying one's personal demons—or who wishes to help others slay theirs—will find this book invaluable."

Brad and Sherry Steiger
Authors of *Real Miracles, Divine Intervention, and Feats of Incredible Survival, Totems,* and many other books

"First of all, I think it's important to mention that Heal Your Soul History is a type of self-help book which doesn't necessarily force you to accept or know, a religion or spiritual beliefs, in order to find solutions for your questions or challenges, which is what makes this book "work." This self-help book can be considered a spiritual guide to everyday living, yet it will make you reflect upon your development as a person and the development of yourself, or ego, or spirit - however you want to name it.

Heal Your Soul History is loosely written, but it gets to the point and does not necessarily need to be read front to back, but you can jump to points which are interesting or important to you. They are clearly described (identifying a problem/finding solution/ why and how come you feel this way/ preventing issues). From loss and addictions to moving on after breakups and self-acceptance, this book seems to have it all covered!"

Katarzyna Crawford
Good Reads Review

"In my line of work, we have many accouterments and strategies that are meant to help us and others survive day to day experiences as well as life threatening situations. It's refreshing to have an author acknowledge the need for "proper spiritual training" for warriors entering into battle. Battles with demons: not only in the physical but on the spiritual planes as well. We must learn to use those weapons of "energy, compassion, telepathy, and presence" as well as the physical tools at our disposal. I've found in reading both books of the series, that I've begun to utilize some of the tools presented. The "Stop, Look, and Listen" exercise is not only spiritually beneficial, but used in the real world, this strategy has helped me to de-escalate situations, listen to and identify victims underlying fears and needs, and find an inner peace and strength for those times that I have lost focus.

As a graduate student in counseling: the books are helpful and I've recommended them to colleagues. Speaking with consumers who see only doom and despair, I can now provide some comfort and insight for them as well as myself. As a Slayer, I am grateful for this powerful opportunity to understand the many spiritual dimensions that others experience and to have the clear, concise, and from the heart spiritual tools these books provide."

Officer Eric Saavedra
Crisis Intervention Specialist, WPD

"This book will call into question much of what you think you know about life—yours and that of others around you. One reading is not enough. I found myself re-reading passages and gaining new insight into the writing each time. That's not to say that the stories aren't engrossing; but the messages beneath are profound, challenging and well worth a second and third thought. I love the book's 'no excuses' approach to understanding and conquering the demons that plague us."

Mariea Cromer
Attorney

"This book made me laugh out loud! ...the book deals with some really difficult topics, even so, I always felt inspired."

Margay Erne

GoTracee Publishing LLC
240 Laurel Street, Suite 101
Baton Rouge, Louisiana, 70801
www.BeASlayer.com

ISBN: 978-0-9963907-2-9 print book
ISBN: 978-0-9963907-0-5 ebook

Illustrations: Michael J Penn www.michaeljpenn.com
Chakra Illustration Graphics: Tita Peterson
Cover & interior Design: Nelly Murariu www.PixBeeDesign.com
Editing: Eric Lyons Thomas, Kathleen Tracy

Publisher's Cataloging-In-Publication Data
(Prepared by The Donohue Group, Inc.)

Names: Dunblazier, Tracee. | Penn, Michael J., illustrator.
Title: Heal your soul history : activate the true power of your shadow / Tracee Dunblazier ; illustrations: Michael J Penn.
Description: Baton Rouge, Louisiana ; Los Angeles, California : GoTracee Publishing LLC, [2016] | Series: The Demon Slayer's handbook series ; [2] | Includes bibliographical references.
Identifiers: LCCN 2016907950 | ISBN 978-0-9963907-2-9 | ISBN 978-0-9963907-0-5 (ebook)
Subjects: LCSH: Self-realization--Religious aspects. | Reincarnation. | Spiritual healing. | Karma. | | Suffering.
Classification: LCC BF1275.S44 D862 2016 (print) | LCC BF1275.S44 (ebook) | DDC 133.9--dc23

Printed in China

THE DEMON SLAYER'S HANDBOOK SERIES

Heal Your Soul History

Activate the True Power of Your Shadow

Tracee Dunblazier

GoTracee Publishing LLC
Baton Rouge, Louisiana Los Angeles, California

Dedication

This book is dedicated with tremendous gratitude to the courageous demon slayers who came before; to the slayers who continue to access, innovate, and express all that the Creator has given them; and to all slayers to come, whose ingenuity will transform this world as we know it, not just because they can but because they must. The journey out of darkness is rich with the obligation of love. An obligation we will all inevitably surrender to. Love is the way and the reward.

Acknowledgements

I've always considered myself lucky, to have what I need when I needed it, in such a magical way. Now, I recognize what I defined as luck was my awareness of the Creators offerings to me. The more I was willing to receive the more I was given. That was the gift of this book to me.

I'd like to thank God's offerings—my family, living and in spirit; the spiritual warriors with whom I have worked; my friends, support, and crew: Doreen, Margay, Lisa, Faith, Sammie, Kathleen, Tita, Jean Marie, Naomi, Jorge, Mariea, Kristine, Mike, Eric, Nelly, Kathleen T., Sara, Jennifer, Google, and Apothic Red—for the boundless humor and hilarity provided daily, the enormous support from long drives and conversations, meals together sharing stories, and the trust that was placed in me by sharing your resources on all levels.

May the blessings rain down on you like never before, and may your open heart receive them effortlessly.

Tracee Dunblazier

Foreword

Judging from the great number of requests for help in freeing individuals from demonic attack that we receive daily, Tracee Dunblazier is answering a need that those afflicted by negative entities are desperately seeking. In *Heal Your Soul History: Activate the True Power of Your Shadow*, Tracee reveals a great number of methods ancient and modern, tribal and urban, that she has employed both to stand her ground in the face of personal demonic attack and that she has utilized to release others from the soul-devouring grasp of parasitic invaders. The book is filled with dramatic case histories. Tracee time and again demonstrates her familiarity with a vast number of spiritual practices and techniques. Written in a style that is personable and easy to read, we think that any reader who is in need of assistance of slaying one's personal demons—or who wishes to help others slay theirs—will find this book invaluable.

Brad and Sherry Steiger

Authors, *Real Miracles, Divine Intervention,*
and *Feats of Incredible Survival*

Contents

Preface

Fight the Devil and Win: One Demon at a Time

All of my experiences in this life have been connected to echoes of untapped pain from past centuries. Pain doesn't go away with time; it patiently waits until it can be exorcised and transformed into something different, something better.

Pain holds your soul together and follows you from incarnation to incarnation awaiting your attention. It is this process that cultivates compassion and opens your heart. As a spiritual empath, when the opportunity came for my heart to break open and let out some of that ancient pain, I took a deep breath, closed my eyes, and let my vocal cords take over.

It is my divine privilege to experience the healing of many incarnations of injustice within myself and to facilitate that same experience for others. I find that nothing strikes fear in people more than what they don't understand and can't control or (at the very least) can't find some humor in.

Fear and Courage

Fear and courage go hand in hand and both came in abundance for me. In fact, I've learned that you cannot have one without the other. When I think back on the many profound experiences of my spiritual journey within my life so far, the much larger picture becomes clear to me and seems so simple.

There has never been a time in this life that I have been confused about who I truly am. The one constant theme is courage that overtakes fear, clarity that commandeers confusion, and ugliness that always gives way to beauty. So in retrospect, my garden path of brick became golden right before my eyes. My life, and the main events that dotted it, no longer provoked self-pity but rather laughter from the irony.

The rhythm goes something like this: My father died when I was eleven, virginity raped from me at eighteen, moved to a New York City ghetto instead of going to college at Texas Christian University, and finally moving to Los Angeles and ending up with a career as a psychic. Trust me, I know how easy it is to judge.

For me, spirit is visibly palpable, but for others spirit is merely imagination, making healing very difficult. It is in this gap in perception where I started to understand why some people do not heal and how I needed to. Healing is a journey, not a judgement against you if you don't believe in what you can't see, or if you see things you just can't believe. I wrote this book to create the opportunity for all of us to expand our awareness and experience of spirit.

In the process of healing, our culture doesn't always begin at the origin of a life pattern. We often stick to the symptoms caused by the pattern, because we've been taught to fear what we are not familiar with.

I found that I couldn't heal completely on all levels without taking a look at the origins of fear. Understanding the function of fear—it is a tool to assist in staying alive, in keeping my body intact, and in keeping my spirit attached to my body in this reality—was vital. With this new understanding, I conceptualized what it would be like to begin to create the tools necessary to live and what the potential results might be, ultimately bringing me around to loving myself unconditionally, accepting others as they are, and being demon free.

It was prophesied by many that the decades proceeding the year 2012—the end of the Mayan calendar's 25,000-year cycle—would bring many trials and tribulations. The end times, they said, would lead us to a completely new world. The Bible talks about the final battles with the devil as being battles with principalities.

The tribulations of the Mayans and the battles in the Book of Revelation are symbols of what I recognized in this modern age as the struggle for *self.* I didn't need to prove my theory, whether it be that ghosts exist, that conspiracies are real, or that God and the devil do or do not exist. What I had to do was find the information that would create the space and allow me to heal mentally, emotionally, and spiritually but most of all, to understand the spirit, mind, body connection so that I could remain healthy. I found that my spiritual and emotional wellness supported or directly and immediately impacted my daily health.

Growing up, nobody wanted to talk about the difficult or profound stuff. Certainly, there weren't any books that could talk about demons, sex, death, and drugs. Those were all the experiences, fears, and imprints that I struggled with all before the age of eleven. One of the things I know is that when you're facing the devil head-on, or running for your life, fear is your friend—but not completely. Your fear will eventually turn on you.

Every day we carry images, energies, strategies, hopes, and dreams of times gone-by. These can take hold in the subtle bodies of our energy field and stay with us for lifetimes. Through my own spiritual journey I have relied on parts of myself, tools of my personality, people who have lived inside of me, and lifetimes I've lived before.

It doesn't matter how I describe them; they are all the elements of my wholeness that make me a unique expression of the divine. Through the *ripped from Tracee's headlines* stories and the exercises of realization that I've created in this work, it's my hope you will find breakthrough moments for your spirit and gain understanding that is relevant to knowing what makes you a unique expression of the Creator.

Writing this book has proven to be quite a challenge as I do not have a lot of memory, no doubt a byproduct of doing this work for as many years as I have. As an empath, I mostly have a catch and release policy; when working with clients, I listen and then grieve their experiences so that I don't retain them for any length of time.

Although I have access to everything I've experienced intuitively, I really just don't remember some things. Doing shamanic work requires that I set aside myself for a little while and carry the spirit of someone else. There have been times when I have felt the grief of thousands. I believe that I am able to work as a spiritual empath because I accept my immense power as a spiritual being while recognizing that I am human and need specific things in order to recover from my spiritual and emotional journeys.

Having said all of that, this book is written without the benefit of notes providing the exact names, dates, and places. What I do have is the spiritual essence, emotional memory, and divine message of each and every experience that I have ever had, whether it is mine or someone else's.

Don't get me wrong: some things I remember as if it were five minutes ago, but I have decided to write the anecdotes commemorated here from the perspective of their purpose and perceived facts rather than a biographical account of each person's story. All of the names and defining details of each story have been changed to preserve any right to privacy, and what is left is the spiritual meaning and teaching of the anecdote. One of the things I have recognized over the years is that people truly hear first what they believe, and secondly, maybe they hear the facts. So it is my hope that you find interest in these stories and see some of yourself within them.

You may read each volume of the series in any order. Each part in a volume contains a parable or story from my personal spiritual history of a spirit guide or past life. The five parables of *Master Your Inner World: Embrace Your Power with Joy* are the stories of the spirit guides that have worked with me in this lifetime and for some over many lifetimes. A spirit guide is a being who's in spirit and a mentor here to be of service to you for a lifetime or through specific experiences and transitions in your life. They've been my teachers and companions through the darkness and into the light. They stood by me in every battle, showing me how to fight the devil and win.

The five parables of *Heal Your Soul History: Activate the True Power of Your Shadow* are of actual, past lifetimes that my spirit has lived; and I have relived them in this lifetime by processing out the emotional memory that I carried. In telling their story, it was important for me to be historically accurate about the history and social mores of the times, but unnecessary to prove the existence of the specific people.

The purpose of telling these stories is to give them all the voice of justice and truth that they all suffered so greatly to receive. All of the details of spiritual sentiment and experiences were channeled from each of the main characters in each story while the names and specific details were inspired by them but given by me for symbolic purposes. Dreams, visions, and events triggered the past memories, and each illustration was created from how each of them presented to me.

Please don't be thrown by the graphic nature of the parables and stories. I understand that not everyone has a life as traumatic as the ones I have depicted, but in fact some do. It will be important to call on the meaning and understanding of each spiritual dynamic inherent in each story, and figure out how it applies to you. There is no reality, only perception. I write this book as an opportunity for you—not to take my truth as your own, but to allow my truth to light up yours and reflect back all that the Creator has given you, to ease your suffering, and to help you experience deep and complete spiritual healing, knowing that when the spirit heals all other levels will follow.

In this book you may find that I use a word that traditionally carries a particular meaning, but I have used it with a different understanding or connotation. My goal here is not to rewrite the English language, but to do my best to convey the depth of these ideas in the simplest way possible, while having reverence for the wordsmiths who have come before me.

It is my intrinsic belief that people are always smarter and wiser and less fearful than they act like they are. This belief has made me always dig deeper within myself and look further into others for the thumping of the eternal heart.

When you know what I know, you can't be a bigot or a racist, a victim or a perpetrator; you can't believe that there is only one path to the Creator, or that death is real.

Most of all, I know we are all of the same essence and that you know what I know somewhere hidden in the secret of your past, present, and future. Somewhere deep within yourself lies the mystery of *wyrd*.[1] You can only be a part of all that is.

1 Fate or destiny

Introduction

A Matter of Spirit

No matter the state of darkness or light, everything has a purpose; those who seek to understand this purpose will find an easy justice. Whether or not you believe in demons, entities, ghosts, earth-bound spirits, depression, mental illness, or insanity, they are a daily truth for some and will touch all in some way during their lifetime. This is an arena in life where ignorance is not bliss—it's just ignorance. The remedy here is knowledge all the way around, to know yourself, to know truth, and to act with compassion.

One question that I believe deep down we all want to know is how can we as individuals take responsibility and be empowered in our part of the world dynamic?

The answer to this question is a matter of spirit. It is common to make the assumption that spiritual matters are religious matters. They are not one and the same. Religion is the spiritual ritual that aligns us with our spirit and our relationship with the Creator; it is not the relationship itself.

In order for all of us to progress, we must acknowledge ourselves as energetic/ spiritual beings. It is unnecessary that we be religious but imperative that we be spiritual. We must acknowledge that our physical body is very dense energy. As the frequency rises the energy patterns become faster and more subtle but not less powerful.

Our energy body, emotions, and thoughts are all forms of this *less dense* matter. All of these forms of matter are propelled by the faster frequencies of energy that preceded them. So when you want to heal completely, you must go to where the energy pattern started the formation of matter in its most subtle, spiritual form.

In the modern world, we don't care what you believe, or what you call your beliefs. We just require that you are willing to give a name to your personal struggle. Here, the devil is all the expressions of illusion that exist, from imagination to the formation of constructs and demons. The devil's only goal is to exist, and its role in this book is that of the all-pervasive, multipurpose antagonist.

Every person's experience of the devil is different, and I believe that the more we all understand each other's experience, the less we will have the need to stay in judgment or impose our ways onto others. The truth in our lives reveals the paths we will take on our journey of perception; truth is the central theme of our spiritual development. It is the destination everyone seeks. It has many faces and stages, and can be loving and kind, or harsh and formidable. Our perception of truth is the only true adversary.

Exploring the five basic levels of perception—physical, etheric, emotional, mental, and causal—is very important because each has a very specific point of reference. This book is about people experiencing all their many parts. It is about witnessing, persevering, enduring, and believing in our ability to heal completely and fully on all levels.

In essence, it is about recognizing our wholeness.

Healing can at times be a progression and at other times may appear to be instantaneous. Learning to accept healing starts with a willingness to accept the illusions we carry about ourselves and others, whether they be ancient or newly born. Accepting your fear, accepting your love, accepting your desire for the information that your illusions bring here and now—all this allows your illusions to be a part of the natural world.

The natural world is the place where all things end or truly begin. The natural world has the final say as to when and how any thought, idea, or concept becomes physically manifest. Spirit, energy, and creativity are all manifestations of our oneness, the Creator, and they eventually become atoms and molecules.

The parts of our spiritual world that will become manifest in our physical world are the places we put our focus. In between your perception of the worlds of spirit and matter, there is a gap where all energy flows. Whatever you believe fills the gap. Whatever you fear fills the gap. Whatever you love fills the gap. This is our path to recognize and honor the gap. Good, bad, or indifferent, all things are sacred.

Accepting where you are today gives you power, the ability to make another decision. If you are fearful of making a decision, accepting that fear as a part of your reality can place you in a position to embrace that fear. If you embrace your fear of committing to an idea, then you are able to access, modify, or innovate what you need in order to create change.

Instead of doing nothing, tell yourself: *Just for today, I will use discipline. Just for today, I will commit to the task at hand. If I want to change my mind tomorrow I can, but just for today I will commit.*

Once you have modified your experience in any way, the dynamic changes. Changing the dynamic every day leads to thought innovation, and as thought innovation sets in, the option for fear has changed completely. This book will address some of the historical belief systems that exist about the human struggle; the spiritual process of their origins, including mental illness, demons, addiction, and sexuality; and how negative thinking is the Creator's message to you in dark times.

The spiritual process is the series of steps each of us must have gone through, are going through, or will go through, in order first to understand the purpose of the spiritual patterns we have been encoded with, and secondly to begin integrating the results of that understanding into our wholeness.

As an empath, it is my expertise to live in the world of illusion and delusion and to master the recognition of the creation of the physical world by witnessing the entire process of emotional perception.

Brain research now shows that perception is a fundamental building block of decision-making. Emotions such as anger, grief, humiliation, disappointment, and confusion are some of the dynamics that will be looked at, understanding that each emotion can be interpreted based on the layer of energy that one focuses through, and that each emotion can have several meanings.

> Did you know that in the Mandarin language, one word can have several meanings? The word ma, for example, has four different meanings based on the intonation that you use to pronounce the word: one intonation means mother and another intonation means dog...There is a lot of room for error here, as there is with the emotional perception of others.

What something means to me is based on the lens that I am looking through. If you don't know or understand my lens, then you don't know my meaning. Through the reinterpretation of difficult feelings, you will begin to innovate your own thoughts, which will allow you to be more intuitive when it comes to understanding others.

Master Your Inner World: Embrace Your Power with Joy also speaks about fear, how you feel when you experience fear, and that through naming the fear gives you a definitive way to address it so that it is changed forever.

Planetary change requires us to shift on all levels: physically, energetically, emotionally, mentally, and spiritually. Through global warming, fracking, and other disruptions caused by humanity, we experience earthquakes, tsunamis, and other natural events on our planet. Humanity *en masse* experiences these same changes internally. In the natural rhythm of this spiritual integration, an identifiable process occurs. When we can recognize our place in this process we are better able to navigate our evolution through understanding ourselves.

An old adage, *water seeks its own level,* describes the spiritual concept of the lowest common denominator. Every person has a lowest common denominator, the part of themselves that is of the densest frequency, such as feelings of lack, hate, grief, inferiority, etc. This lowest common denominator can't vibrationally shift until the self has gone through a process of spiritual evolution. And, the lens in which he looks through has been transformed or raised up to another, more expansive, form of seeing and experiencing life. The lowest common denominator can be found in all layers of the mind, body, and spirit.

Choice is the first tool to master. It begins with the concept that the consciousness of every human being is made of a *high self, middle self,* and *low self.* In this model, the higher self is the highest frequency we have access to. The middle self is the cognizant mind while the low self is all of the energy that is contained in our spirit—or as I refer to it, *the gap*.

When the conscious mind decides to do something, it makes its request to the higher self. Prior to success, all the information in the spirit is scanned to determine what obstacles exist to the manifestation of the idea. All focus will then move to the lowest common denominator of the energy or the most formidable obstacle. Discerning what beliefs or ideologies can stay and support the emerging idea, or which ones need to be recycled.

If we have beliefs that won't allow for the manifestation of our desire, then our choices are likely to match our beliefs and not our desires. We now know what belief systems we have in place that are not in alignment with what we want, and we can choose to give them up and adopt new ones that match our goals.

Many spiritual philosophies hold a concept known as the *holy death*, which refers to a death or completion of the spirit. When death occurs in any situation, it marks the end of one dynamic and the beginning of a new one. If we acknowledge that all things are created of spirit, then spirit would be the place to go to make changes to those creations.

What it takes to heal

Healing requires a relentless desire to heal, unequivocal commitment and devotion to the process, and a complete trust in the deepest parts of yourself for having created the conflict (on a spiritual level) in the first place. It is only through brutal honesty—and a few laughs—that we can heal ourselves and this planet. I hope that this book will be the beginning of that process for others as it has been for me.

Everyone has his or her own ghosts of events passed, of people wronged, of the irrevocable choices made by you or affecting you. No matter how these energies present themselves, or the paradigm with which you look at them, they are there and can be reconciled in some way. You do not have to continue to live with them. They can be transformed and healed when you recognize their purpose. This book, while truthful, is not designed to be *the* truth, but to mirror the reader's truth back to them. The sections of each chapter are connected with one another in terms of meaning and understanding, but the logic is not exact and linear.

Whether or not the concept of past lives is a part of your belief system is irrelevant here; what is true is that we all carry with us imprints of spiritual knowledge that, when processed, awaken in us a truth, wisdom, and understanding about ourselves.

These imprints of spiritual knowledge convey to us a dynamic that both no longer serves us and includes the way out of the old dynamic, all in one package. These imprints are called the Akashic records, our soul's personal lineage of how we know all that we know. The Akashic records oftentimes offer us the opportunity to grieve what was left behind, and—through the action of grief—create space in the brain to affirm a new dynamic all the way down to the biochemical level.

Each chapter includes several sections: *The Slayer's Weapons, The Slayer's Path, The Slayer's Motto, The Slayer's Pact,* and *The Slayer's Altar* (or *Ritual*).

- *The Slayer's Weapons* are positive or negative dynamics that we all experience, such as joy or self-pity. It is through these dynamics that the Slayer is able to witness herself and others and learn about her deepest spiritual expression, transforming her patterns and environment.
- *The Slayer's Path* gives a concept that helps the slayer align with their truth during the particular phase of development that the Slayer may be experiencing.
- *The Slayer's Motto* is a tagline or affirmation that a slayer can repeat over and over again to remind themselves of their chosen path.
- *The Slayer's Pact* is a unifying idea that all slayers commit to on their journey.
- And finally, *the Slayer's Altar* or *Ritual* is the physical world completion that cements the slayer's commitment to overcome any deeply rooted pervasive energy and then to heal on every level.

The information in the chapters will educate you about demons and all the spiritual dynamics that we humans can be affected by. You will learn things like who and what demons are, where they live, how they were created, and how and why they function as they do.

You will also be illuminated as to what you already have, and what you need to have, in order to commence victory over every one of them. You will gain an understanding of your personal spiritual tools that you've brought into this life and the dynamics within you that are being healed.

The anecdotes in this book are inspired by real life accounts but are in no way accurate to anyone's exact experience. I've created them to illustrate in a defined way the specific spiritual dynamics that I believe are the most valuable and necessary for this teaching.

Again, the elements of the book are interactive and can include information that connects with any of the parables and stories. The purpose of this design is for you the reader to be able to access your own personal stories and truths through the process of working through this book.

Finally, each chapter is my personal story, containing some of the events, past-life visions, and spiritual experiences that illuminated my soul guides and stories. I have always been empathic, psychic, and fully aware of my spiritual knowledge, even from as early as my days in the crib. I don't think I am unique in this experience, and I believe that many of our world citizens today are opening up to their own personal knowledge or are born with the empathetic awareness of their gifts, or *tools* as I prefer to call them.

This book offers strategies for balancing life's traumas and dares us to have the audacity to laugh and see the world through someone else's eyes. A spiritual perspective coupled with real-life accounts, mixed with how-tos and how-not-tos, will be helpful to those who are willing to help themselves.

In our culture today there is a lot of focus on all that we have lost and are losing. As I contemplated it, we're bringing light to even darker and denser places in our spirits and in our world.

It is my hope that everyone within the sound of my voice will seek their truth and that through this book all readers will embrace and face their demons whatever they may be, gaining a deeper understanding of themselves, others, and the way the universe works. Finally, I hope that you will know that grief and suffering are simply a part of the spiritual process of being beautiful and peaceful, and that peace is inevitable for everyone who makes the effort.

Please feel free to work with this book however you are guided to. Read it in order, out of order, only parts of it, or in whatever way you need in order to metabolize the right information at the right time.

And if you've been led to this book, then without a doubt it has something for you or for someone you know. So go forth and conquer.

PART ONE

DON'T SURRENDER

Demons are Liars

The Slayer's Weapons:

Forgiveness, Apathy, Depression,
Foresight, Patience

Leaving the Past in the Past: Forgiveness

The slayer has many weapons in their arsenal—sometimes apparently positive and obvious, at times negative and mysterious, but weapons just the same. Apathy is the beginning practice leading to neutrality, while depression requires a deeper level of self-exploration. Leaving the past in the past is not always such an easy or immediate task for everyone. Sometimes our present life is fraught with echoes of our past lives reverberating goodness and prosperity, or pain and suffering, in every breath we take. The five chapters of this volume each contain the story of a past life that I lived. Spiritually, I brought each of these past-life imprints with me in order to deliver myself from the pain and tumult I experienced in that existence. The processing of each past life in this current one required me to relive those profound memories accompanied with a torrent of grieving.

I have given each one of my soul's incarnations a voice not previously heard and the forgiveness that she deserves. In this context, the forgiveness is the actual letting go of the memory, dynamic, and energy pattern from having lived through the experiences. Today, reawakening them in my conscious mind in order to reclaim my freedom. It's been necessary to forgive both myself and all those souls—whether they were friend or foe at the time—with whom I shared those life events.

Forgiveness means completely grieving and letting go. I have given each one of these ladies a name and done my best to interpret the channeling of their stories and the essence of the events in their lives. It's not been my goal to prove their existence, but to process the pain and capture the wisdom that was indelibly linked and so richly won through their hard-earned characters.

The Story of Higuemota Guevara

The darkness was stiff, yet comforting. The crispness of the ocean air and the subtle rock of the midnight waves somehow brought a lullaby to my pain. I have such grief and shame it makes it hard to tell my story. To know that I have touched and known such evil in humanity makes me feel embarrassed about my faith.

The year is 1509. I am a young woman about the age of seventeen, and my name is Higuemota. You would think it would matter that I was born of a cacique[1] and an heir to the leadership of my proud Taino people. The conquistadores that came to ravage my tribe are so hateful. I was stolen after a great massacre and raped over and over again on a great ship by a Spaniard who wanted to use me as his wife. I am impregnated from the encounters. All I can remember are the smells so abundant and foul. It was as if I could smell the hate in his perspiration. I just laid there as if my heart could break no more, but little did I know what was to come: nine agonizing months on that ship with those smells. I was pregnant and waiting for every day to pass.

For some reason they never made me work and occasionally took me to the top deck for some fresh air. The daily darkness was not my friend. It ate away at my faith every minute. Even the spirit of my beloved mother could not get to me, her spirit shut out by the darkness that enveloped me every moment that passed. Now this help I prayed for was slipping away as I fell deeply into my futility. Even with this life growing inside of me, I wanted no future, only liberation. The gentle smell of the sea water was no longer comforting. The last prayer I made was for strength, it wouldn't be long now.

The dark one came to me on a particularly stormy night. I knew what it was, but I didn't care. It repeated over and over that nothing mattered and there was no way out. I felt nothing as I listened; by this time I was numb. It kept beckoning me to follow it, telling me that there was nothing for me here. It helped me up out of the place where I slept and onto the top deck, and—before I had time to think about it—I and my unborn child were right over the rail. The water was ice-cold and it wasn't long before I had the liberation I had been yearning for. My lifeless body fell deep to the ocean floor, soft and nestled in the arms of Yaya.[2]

> I found my connection and salvation at the Brooklyn Bridge, helping desperate, isolated souls who felt they had no other alternative but to jump.

1 chief
2 The supreme Taino spirit

I made the only obvious choice I could with my limited range of view. I could not spend another minute with that cruel man and his people and those smells. I couldn't bare the loss of my mother and my family. I felt no sadness for me or the unborn life I carried, only resentment of the hatred of the man and the seed he left inside me. I had believed the liberation from my worldly constraints would bring light, but it only brought more confusion. The spirit of my baby was now gone. Even the dark spirit that had been with me on the boat, was gone. I was alone completely; it wasn't supposed to be this way. My spirit, now free—floating in the ocean full of resentment, confusion, and fear—wandered for years in the ocean's darkness.

Eventually, I found a pod of dolphins. Swimming with them every day and night for what had become centuries taught me just how narrow my view had been, guided by rage. The dolphins invited me into their family and taught me with their constant migration a different understanding of eternal life. Now, if I could breathe, I'd laugh. This is not to say that I don't remember the darkness and the resentment. It held on for at least two hundred years. But now, with me swimming in the peaceful waves of acceptance, I can see another path for that life.

The vision of an alternative path could have only come in this way, without words or a time limit: beyond liberation, the real freedom and light came from helping others. At first, it was succoring the occasional sailor who lost his life at sea or bringing comfort to the passengers of a ship capsized during a violent storm.

While following the migration path of the dolphins from the mid-Atlantic all the way up to the northeast coast of North America, the cities seemed to industrialize right before my eyes. And, as the world became more modern with the building of bridges, I found my connection and salvation at the Brooklyn Bridge with isolated souls who felt they had no other alternative but to jump. I helped them in the hope that their spiritual recovery wouldn't take centuries as mine had and that they would be able to reunite with the great love as soon as possible. On most occasions I helped a spirit to find the light and be liberated, but one experience allowed me the privilege of helping a weary woman transition her grief and fear into bravery and courage. It was the end of the Great Depression and signs of the Second World

War were imminent. I found her climbing over the railing getting ready to jump but holding on in hesitation.

I rose up to stand beside her and whispered in her ear, "It doesn't have to be this way."

In anger, she said to me, "Why does God let these things happen? Why doesn't he just take us all and let this end?"

I replied, "Maybe he will. Maybe that will be for the best, but for now take a moment to think about this. Since you are not afraid of death anyway, wouldn't it be interesting to see if you could change things for yourself with only your will. It seems that your belief dictates that God can change everything? So aligning with that would allow *you* to change anything, right? Wouldn't that be an interesting experiment, to see if you could? You have nothing to lose since the next step is death anyway. What if you could come together in God's name, and your will be done?"

I continued: "I know you feel alone, so consider me in. I'll align with you and your will be done. Wouldn't *that* be interesting enough to stay around, just to see if you, aligning with the Creator, can make a new life happen for yourself? I mean, ultimately, you can have all the time in the world to figure it out in the afterlife, but wouldn't it be interesting to get it when you still have a living body?"

Her weeping stopped, and she said, "I can't see you."

"But nonetheless you can hear me and know I am here; know that you are not alone."

She said, "I don't know how."

"Okay," I said, "Well, let's get you off of this bridge for starters."

> IT IS CERTAIN THAT THE UNIVERSE IS ONE OF CONTINUOUS CHANGE. NO OBSERVER CAN HESITATE TO ADMIT WHAT IS SO EVIDENT TO ALL. DEVELOPMENT NEVER CEASES ITS ENDLESS ROUND OF OPERATIONS.
>
> NATHAN R. WOOD

The Suicide Demons are Formidable

The suicide demons' greatest tool is apathy. Demons want you to believe that there is no way out, no matter what you do. If they can in any way keep you feeling futile about your condition or situation, then they can keep you bound to what plagues you. Being a demon slayer I've not ever considered suicide. I can't say that I don't comprehend it because I do and always have in some ways, but the one thing I've always clung to in times of immense darkness was knowing I would never take that action.

Yet, there was a period of time when things had been weighing on me, heavier by the day. I knew I was surrounded by a darkness I couldn't quite describe, and I didn't know where it came from. I was afraid to go to sleep at night, or be by myself during the day. After weeks of this the anxiety and fear whose origin I could not see gave way to complete, all-encompassing apathy; and that's when the demonic assaults to my mind began.

Nighttime was the worst. For about five days nonstop, the demons' voices created a chatter in my mind: *What's the point? None of this matters. No one really cares. Just kill yourself.*

Within my complete numbness, it made sense. Maybe I *should* kill myself. There really *isn't* any point. I'm *never* going to get out from under all this. Dying would *free* me. I'm going to come back anyway. I *should* kill myself.

What?!

A small, faint thought in my mind said: *You can't fight this and you can't hear it.*

My mind was so jumbled and confused that I couldn't think straight enough to pray, so I chanted Christ's name over and over...*Christ, Christ, Christ.* I did this for hours, until I fell asleep. This went on every night, while every day I made sure to be around someone every minute.

I tried to speak about what was happening to one friend who cavalierly said, "Don't worry, you got this," and changed the subject.

Nobody really wanted to hear about the depth of this darkness around me, and certainly no one expected *me* to be impacted. Finally, on the fifth day, I left the house as soon as I got up. I didn't have anyone to babysit me that day so I went to the coffee shop where I sat nursing a cup of coffee until I ran into a friend, Melvin. He took one look at me, and he knew.

He said, "Come spend the day with me. I've got some errands to run."

And I did. We didn't speak much, and we didn't talk about *it*. I was relieved that someone knew what I was going through, and for the next twelve hours, I silently went with him from place to place, and by the time he dropped me at my house, the darkness was gone.

Hmmm...but *where* had it gone?

No judgment, only consequences

If you lose or take your own life in this state of apathy, you are in a less powerful position than if you'd stayed in your body. There is a lot of confusion about what happens to the soul of a person who dies of suicide or anguish in some way, so I'd like to clear it up for you. The state a person is in when they die is the state they remain in after death. And it is the lower vibrational states of being—like anguish, fear, anger, grief, bitterness, or hate—that keep a spirit earthbound.

Dying itself won't help to transform those states of being; transformation occurs only by processing them fully. Dying just lessens your power to efficiently process the emotion and change it, but rest assured, in other dimensions of energy, time is irrelevant and surely an earthbound spirit will complete its task eventually.

When a person is murdered or dies in an abrupt manner of some sort, it is often the shock of the experience that may keep them earthbound. Some spirits, no matter the cause of death, stay earthbound in order to help those they've left behind for a period of time. Everyone has some aspects to life that are a part of their destiny, and others that are free will. It is never about the *events* that take place in one's life, but the energetic pattern that is learned and transformed. We are able to transform life patterns that no longer serve us when we are willing to completely understand them from all viewpoints: energetically (considering its impact on others), emotionally (feeling-based), mentally (intellectually and analytically), and spiritually (with compassion, without judgment).

Most often, when a person is going to die there is some sort of consciousness of it, whether the death is unexpected or not. The spirit has an awareness and a plan. Such a person often begins a few months prior to the death event, wrapping up their life in some way, whether or not they or anyone else realizes it. The purpose is to begin to pull back their energy from this world in order to transition to the next. When death is their destiny, cognitive awareness of the end-of-life wrap-up sometimes eludes them and their loved ones.

Greyson's story

A few years ago, an old high school friend of mine had the unthinkable happen. It was New Year's Day of 2011, and her eighteen-year-old son Greyson had gone out for the evening and arrived home just after midnight, safe and sound. With a sigh of relief and a smile she said goodnight and goodbye to another good year. She found his lifeless body in his bed at noon the next day. He'd taken some prescription drugs with his friends and accidentally overdosed. Devastating doesn't even cover it. How could this have happened? He was an amazing kid who was a star football player and about to graduate high school.

His mother Dana and I had become reacquainted on social media and didn't know each other all that well in high school as she'd been my sister's friend. Out of the blue, my sister called and told me what'd happened to Dana's son and asked if I had any information. I didn't but said I'd check. Immediately, while still on the phone with my sister, I saw a young man in my mind's eye. I didn't know him and his energy was faint. He felt very far away from me, but I suspected it was Dana's son. Throughout the rest of the evening, I couldn't get him out of my mind, but his energy was still quite faint. As I pondered, it made sense as he was newly transitioning, and I didn't have any substantial connection with him or his family except through my sister's relationship with his mom—and they'd not had contact in years. I acknowledged him and then he disappeared.

Learning of the circumstances of his death and his ability to so quickly make contact with me, I knew he was on a mission of some sort. I expected it would only be a matter of time before Dana called. Over the next few months he visited me frequently, getting stronger in his ability to communicate with me, and more frustrated that I couldn't call his mom. He didn't understand why I just wouldn't reach out to her. I explained to him that her call to me was inevitable, but that it had to come in her time and when she was ready.

He expressed frustration because he'd tried several times to communicate with her and other family members, but didn't feel he was getting through. I reassured him that he was connecting on some level, but grief sometimes clouds the bridge to a persons awareness of the spiritual dimension he was in. Finally, he came to me in a dream and woke me up. It was about two in the morning, and I knew she'd made contact. Sure enough I got up and checked my email, and there was a note from her. She told me the story and asked if we could set up a session. Greyson and I were relieved. When the appointed day came, he woke me up early. Earthbound spirits don't always have awareness of our time frame in their world, but this kid was a go-getter. He'd been cultivating his message for his mother for a few months now and was ready and excited like it was the first day of school.

> HIS LEGACY WAS BEING A TRUE FRIEND, LIVING IN THE MOMENT, AND HIS PASSION FOR FOOTBALL.
>
> DANA NEWAN

Dana and I started out with the pleasantries, but cut them short as Greyson was eager. He started out by explaining how sorry he was for what happened. It never occurred to him that he could lose his life by experimenting with drugs. He loved her very much and wanted her to use her grief to help people. He knew he no longer had his body, but he was by no means gone. He felt so sad for his mother and the other family and friends, it was heart-breaking to watch them grieve his loss. He was beginning to understand that bigger things could come from what happened. He felt like his mom could help many people through his story and her voice through the grief.

Dana took her son's request to heart and began a foundation called Greyson's Legacy in order to raise awareness of teen recreational use of prescription medication and the thousands of teens who were losing their lives in accidental overdoses all over the country.

"I eventually asked that the Greyson's Legacy website be taken down as I feel that it is not his legacy as much as it is mine," she explains. "His legacy was being a true friend, living in the moment, and his passion for football. It is hard to constantly associate your child's name with overdose as he was *so much* more than how he died. It is my journey to share this as a parent: how easily it can happen and remove judgment, shame, and stigma. I don't want this to define him. He is an amazing young man that got caught up in something bigger than he ever suspected. My work now is with an organization called Healing Addiction in our Community. I call it channeling my grief and a place to put all of this energy associated with my grief."

Today, Dana remains a public voice for the awareness of this issue and a reminder of the beautiful life of her son Greyson.

The Slayer's Path: If You Can't Move Forward, Step to the Side

Sometimes a slayer, when confronted with what appears to be impenetrable circumstances, must change course by stepping one foot in any direction and trusting that this modest action will change the known path. To really explore your self-trust, it is important to conceptualize the process of the soul's reawakening. We are born with all the information that we will ever need in our lifetime. The exciting part is the reawakening to it all, and then applying it differently this time.

When we feel victimized the natural reaction is to victimize others by fighting through the struggle. The victim/ perpetrator dynamic is, in essence, what we call duality: light/dark, good/evil, joy/sadness, or conscious/unconscious. Feeling victimized is a phase of spiritual development. When we are in it and aren't able to innovate the current pattern, we call it *addiction*. If you add additional perspectives to that equation, then you are no longer going in the same direction. It only takes a small movement in any direction to change course.

Identifying your patterns

To find your patterns, all you have to do is look at what you notice outside of yourself. What you think everyone else is doing to you is what you are doing to yourself. The recovery community has a saying: *You spot it, you got it.*

When you take note of a characteristic in someone else, in the spiritual phase of ignorance, you are actually recognizing something about yourself in some way. What you judge or appreciate in someone else, you are judging or appreciating in yourself. We call it *mirroring*. At any given time, we are experiencing different spiritual themes or energetic patterns in our lives. All we have to do to recognize them is to pay attention, think, and feel.

Ignorance is the beginning of the conscious mind's acknowledgment of the spiritual pattern that guides it. For example, if you are a person who sees yourself as always doing for others, and them not doing for you, then in what ways are you not doing for yourself?

What is addiction?

The definition of addiction for our purposes today is a seemingly insatiable compulsive need to do the same thing over and over again desiring a new result and disregarding the consequences. This compulsion does not necessarily need to be for substances like drugs or alcohol; it can be any behavior that has been proven to bring unfortunate consequences.

Brain research has proven that our habits form our neurological circuitry, the elements of the brain that help us to process and remember information. Conversely, practicing new behavior helps us to create and populate new circuitry with new information to form new habits. The brain's plasticity (ability to change) is proof that almost any behavior can be changed with effort. The greatest carrier of change from our spirit to our brain is emotion. Emotional energy can change, block, or support the way we relate or interpret something. We are beginning to see research proving that our neural circuitry is an integral part of the physiology that helps us recognize our feelings. As an empath, I believe that our emotional energy is generated from our spirit. Our emotion helps us to recognize and define the information within our spirit; however this has yet to be proven by science.

Modern neuroscience has shown that certain emotions—like joy, fear, surprise, shame, disgust, anger, and sadness, to name a few—have their own brain pathways and chemicals and affect us on every level, including the creation of inflammation in the body that can lead to illness and disease. Emotion interprets meaning, so we remember information that is brought to us through intense emotional responses. Our spiritual experiences create emotions; emotions drive our thoughts, decisions, and finally, our choices.

> POWER IS AT THE ROOT OF THE HUMAN EXPERIENCE. OUR ATTITUDES AND BELIEFS—POSITIVE OR NEGATIVE—ARE ALL EXTENSIONS OF HOW WE DEFINE AND USE POWER.
>
> CAROLINE MYSS

Defying your emotions

Learning to respond in spite of your emotions is a part of the final phase of spiritual process called *completion*. Up until this point our goal is to learn to use our emotion to interpret a situation, but not to define the actions to be taken. Taking action requires that we begin to retrain our bodies and minds out of the fight-or-flight response and understand the role that emotion plays in our lives from a spiritual perspective.

Spiritual depression is a common occurrence that takes place as a person is learning to take higher-minded actions in spite of how they feel. Spiritual depression is intense spiritual reflection through grief, in relationship to your connection to the Creator or your feeling of separateness from the Creator. Other experts believe it has some distinct differences from clinical depression, which is considered a chronic biological mood disorder. Symptoms include an enduring inability to interact with friends and loved ones, to set aside daily realities to live and appreciate life, or to take care of your basic needs. All these can be indicators of clinical depression.

What distinguishes spiritual from clinical depression is the amount of time one stays in the depressed condition and the body's replication of the biochemical cocktail that renders you depressed. Many people experienced a spiritual depression directly after 9/11, when they asked themselves the deeper questions about their faith in and about their relationship to, the existence of God or their general safety. Once having processed those questions, they were able to move on to the next experiences of their life.

However, as an empath I have lived most of my life in a perpetual dark night of the soul or spiritual depression. There have been times when those spiritual transformations coincided with different hormonal events that left me deeply out of balance emotionally and physically. I've experienced almost every symptom of clinical depression on the list. Although it was suggested to me on multiple occasions that I should see a doctor, I never sought a diagnosis—for obvious reasons. (I didn't want to be labeled for something I knew in my heart I would overcome.) I've always believed that my experiences and symptoms were the reflections of what for many years felt like an endless reign of spiritual pain and untold stories. For me, doing spiritual work was the only possible path, and medication would have only inhibited my spiritual healing. While it has proven to be a profound marathon of long suffering, with each spiritual experience I dug up and transformed, I was ultimately left lighter and more able than before. (I suppose that in the context of many centuries of spiritual experience, forty years is a mere drop in the bucket.)

The Slayer's Path: **If You Can't Move Forward, Step to the Side**

The Slayer's Motto: Asking for Help Makes Me Stronger

Mental illness

Everyone must tend their own garden, no matter the tools used, whether those methods include a Western approach with medication and psychotherapy, spiritual work, emotional processing, behavior modification, or a combination of all of them. You can choose to ask for help directly or receive the help laid in your path from the Creator. No matter the road you take, learning to take care of yourself and your body is a necessity. I am certain I wouldn't be alive today if it weren't for the stringent focus and care I have put towards staying healthy by using modalities like massage therapy, energy medicine, acupuncture/Chinese medicine, and vitamin/herbal supplements.

My core belief is that mental illness is ultimately spiritual imbalance, and the two can in no way be perceived as separate. However, it's important to understand that while dealing with the symptoms of a mental illness, a person's physiological condition—the brain and body—can sometimes prevent any subtle spiritual awareness. It may be impossible to look at the larger spiritual picture because the way someone receives and perceives information isn't connecting to the energy of the heart or the part of the brain that allows for rational thinking and impulse control. In those cases, getting help from a qualified professional is a must, and in some circumstances medication may be required to keep the person and others safe.

> If you kill yourself or someone else kills you, then you will transition to another dimension in the exact condition you were in at the time of death.

What to do if you hear voices telling you to kill

No entity of any sort that has your best interest at heart, will ask you to kill yourself or another. And I feel secure in the knowledge that God will never ask it of you either. If you hear a voice saying, *I am God, and you should kill,* then—whoever it is—the voice is not that of God; the entity is trying to trick you. You should tell them to shut the *@#$%* up. Demons and other entities on occasion will say anything to get you to create more pain and chaos in your world. There is no circumstance in which killing yourself or someone else helps a situation, creates freedom, or reduces pain. If you kill yourself or someone else kills you, then you will transition to another dimension in the exact same condition that you were in at the time of death. It is not uncommon for a person who is murdered to attach to the one who killed them, or to one who killed another, after death.

No shame in asking for help

If voices are telling you to kill, and if you feel vulnerable or apathetic to their constant gnawing at you to hurt yourself or someone else, call 911 first, and then tell those around you that you need help. Calling the emergency line will let the authorities know about your crisis situation, and they will send an ambulance and possibly the police. The ambulance will then take you to a hospital for a seventy-two-hour hold and a psychiatric evaluation to obtain the help you need to get out of the crisis zone.

Always, the first thing to do is to get yourself to a safe place, and then deal with any other spiritual, mental, emotional, or physical issues later. Let me reiterate here that getting help out of the crisis zone is not healing, but only an indication that further work needs to be done, either psychologically (e.g., if you have undiagnosed issues) or spiritually (e.g., in the case of a spiritual attack, to understand what made you vulnerable to the attack in the first place). Make no mistake here: even if it appears that your life has resumed normalcy, there is much work to be done. Don't let anyone or anything shame you into believing otherwise.

The Slayer's Motto: **Asking for Help Makes Me Stronger**

Spiritual death and grief

When we consider our ideas on grief, most people focus on death. As a spiritualist and empath, it is a part of my work to recognize all beginnings and endings as cycles of death and rebirth and to focus on the empirical value of the spiritual process as it relates to our thoughts, emotions, and physical well-being. It is the nature of science to focus on the empirical value of results, not necessarily giving the same value to the process. Both perspectives are necessary for balance to be achieved.

There are many works that have helped to shape our culture's beliefs about grief and our relationship to death and rebirth, and have helped us to transition into a more peaceful place for the dying and present and vibrant place for the living. However, today I believe it's time for another such transition involving the self-awareness that only courage can bring and that allows us to be present in every moment we are living or dying.

Every day, people experience some sort of change. If it's not happening to you, then it's happening to someone you know or in the world you live. Every single one of these changes, large or small, requires a process of transition. They all have an impact, spiritually, mentally, and emotionally; and it is less important whether the change is a catastrophic upheaval or many different simple movements. It is the effect of multiple transitions that creates a challenge for our ability to process them. What we need is to establish a plan for grieving our passages before we must do the work of grief.

A popular sentiment reserves the idea of grief for when someone dies and promotes the denial of our own mortality. We somehow see death or transition as a failure rather than beautiful and inevitable. We must learn to embrace death and other life transformations openly and without fear, to recognize there is a spiritual and emotional process inherent in each change. We can't forget that for every ending there is a new beginning. In addition, we need to acknowledge the impact of the many-layered circumstances that one person can experience, learning to recognize the inevitable emotional and spiritual build up and finding ways of expression that are not only productive, but satisfying.

Crying: Not just for women and babies anymore

For centuries emotionalism has been looked at as a weakness and sometimes even a mental illness. So you may need to change this outlook and recognize that your emotions—especially what we call grief—are really ways that your mind, heart, and spirit are cleansed and replenished for sustained use. Research has proven that crying for ten minutes or more actually changes the neurons in the brain. It is my experience that this is true. It's like grieving erases any attachment that you have to certain memories and sometimes erases the memories themselves. Grieving releases stress and opens the mind and heart to innovative resolutions and change.

> We must learn to embrace death and other life transitions openly and without fear to recognize there is a spiritual and emotional process inherent in each change. We can't forget that for every ending there is a new beginning.

It is a fact that *any* loss—even a happy transition—can elicit a grief response or feelings related to grief. Events like getting married, moving, and buying a new car or home all require the giving up of one thing for another. This requires a transition. It is common to have a sense of guilt or shame about the emotional process of these changes. For some people, it is the unspoken expectation that sadness, or the expression of it, implies weakness. Today's energetic, spiritual, and technological climate on the planet creates an obligation to change. Our increasing spiritual awareness and emotional sensitivity require a different relationship to ourselves. The immediate exchange of information among us requires a shift in how we relate to one another and our emotions.

Over the years, working with so many people, I have witnessed a process that each person goes through while transitioning from one phase to another, beginning spiritually and ending in the physical world with a new result. The *anatomy of change* is a simple breakdown of the seven elements of the spiritual process. Keep in mind these phases aren't necessarily linear and will often overlap.

The Anatomy of Change: The Seven Elements of Spiritual Process

Ignorance is the phase of spiritual process where we start to become aware of the impending change in our lives, seeing it happening to others around us or noticing it in our thoughts, feelings, and environment. However, we don't feel it applies to us, so we ignore it. Pay attention to your thoughts and what you notice: thinking it doesn't apply to you is a signal that you should pay more attention. Ignorance is different from denial: in denial there is no acknowledgment of consciousness, whereas in ignorance you acknowledge the dynamic but don't apply it to yourself.

Resistance is the phase of spiritual process where now the evidence of the change is connecting to our conscious mind through extreme negativity or resistance. Resistance is often signified by phrases like, *I'd never do that* or *That person is so (fill in the blank).* Whatever you are acknowledging through a negative perspective indicates the change that is beginning in your life.

Conflict/Struggle is the phase of spiritual process where we start to engage the possibility of the change, and in preparation we will begin to adopt new philosophies that will support the change. We then begin to release old belief systems, people, circumstances, or things that do not support the change.

Surrender is the phase of spiritual process that acknowledges a release of the old pattern, person, place, or thing, and a discomfort or lack of understanding of what will be taking its place.

Change/Choice is the phase of spiritual process when a decision is made or action taken that makes a significant, irrevocable change. Although any decision that can be made can be changed, you can never un-know what you have learned from the process.

Comedy is the phase of spiritual process that helps us detach from the old and open up to the new. Objectivity through jokes and humor allow us to explore thoughts and feelings about our circumstances without fear. This phase can also bring experiences and perspective that is so foreign to the self they border on the absurd.

Completion is the phase of spiritual process where the new ideas integrate and manifest in the physical. They can manifest as wisdom and understanding, emotional breakthrough, a change in philosophy or beliefs, or receiving something in the physical world. Completion is the time when all questions have been answered and one can truly move on to the next phase. Completion can take years depending on what is being processed, it means we have moved through the dynamic on all levels. Keep in mind, it is our multidimensional nature to be able to process many things at the same time.

The Slayer's Pact: Live Well, Die Easy

Death is a multimillion-dollar industry, and every culture has its rituals for sending the dead into the afterlife. Much time and expense are given to those whom have passed on, and it seems we don't give enough time, attention, or resources in acknowledging the ending of a person's life. The last few months of one's existence is such a beautiful and sacred time, it is my hope that one day we will be free enough in our relationship with death to speak of it easily; and to celebrate every phase of life while are loved ones are still living.

To give you a rough idea, an average funeral costs about $6,500, and in the United States alone there have been close to 2.5 million deaths in a decade, with approximately a quarter of those resulting in cremation. That makes the annual costs for funerals are more than a billion dollars. How would life be for a person in the dying process if we spent that money on them while they were still alive?

> Isn't it time to create space and opportunity to celebrate each other during the final days of life, instead of in the fear or shadow of death itself?

The death industry is for the living. I've spent more than a few hours at some of the Civil War–period cemeteries all over the country and am always in awe of the beauty. Even though some have been ravaged by time and nature, the lush green lawns hold in place the uneasy cracked pieces of concrete bearing the half-worn names of our rich country's descendants. Some of the ironwork is incredibly ornate, with each small grave fence forged to forever mimic something beautiful from the natural world like a leaf or a flower. Now the rusted iron is stronger than the bodies and the gravestones they protected.

One of the most amazing sites was a mausoleum, whose door was virile and ironclad with a huge padlock, while the foundation building was cracked and withered into a pile of bricks. It made me consider how much any one of those things would cost today and what's the purpose they serve? Do any of those folks who died in the 1860s still have people to visit them? Who visited them back in the late nineteenth century and for how long?

In fact, our desire as a society to indulge in the funeral process for the departed is so staggering that entire gravesites have been dug up and the bodies discarded, just to make room to sell plots to newly dead consumers. While these gravesites have been, sometimes, the only connection to our history, I think with the amount of people on the planet (7.1 billion) and in the United States (approximately 320 million) the limited amount of space may just dictate that it's time to make some changes. I saw in the news a few years back that a funeral home had to pay reparations to the families whose plots were dug up. Clearly, the grieving and mourning process, and our relationship to death in general, must be reevaluated. Isn't it time to create space and opportunity to celebrate each other during the final days of life, instead of in the fear or shadow of death itself?

Focusing on the purpose of ritual, rather than on the ritual itself, gives us the change in prospective that is needed to see the patterns, signs, and modalities of transition that are always there. Focusing on the purpose of the ritual can encourage us to live more fully with ourselves and with each other.

Time for life

While I feel that ritual at the end of a life is deeply important for the living and their process of grieving and mourning, I believe a more personal memorialization, via a personal altar or planted tree, is an efficient way to go. It is easily accessible to the grieving, and can be created and called on at any time for very little money, if any. Quite honestly, those who are in spirit can go anywhere. It is not the cost of the funeral that defines a dead person's worth to their loved ones; it is what those loved ones are willing to offer in life.

Remember Slayer's: the devil wants you to stay in loss and the fear of losing again. It's time to put more emphasis on what happens to a person before they transition, rather than on what happens afterward. The few months before a person is going to leave this world, whether the means of departure is known or unknown, are quite sacred and beautiful. I have had the profound opportunity to be called into the lives of many in the few months before they died, whether the death be via homicide, suicide, car accident, overdose, or cancer. The pattern is the same. The people who die from a so-called accidental death (or from another unexpected event) and those who die from the expected effects of a chronic disease, both behave similarly in their final days. Quite simply, they wrap up their lives.

The Slayer's Pact: **Live Well, Die Easy**

A life lived quickly and simply

My twenty-one-year-old colleague Misha and I weren't close; she always seemed so sad. The bitter taste of her attitude and struggle for authority were really hard to swallow, and if truth be told we didn't have much in common in our way of doing things. It was the duty of our job as managers that required our connection and communication, but often I found we had to stretch a bit to get along. She was a little boy-crazy and called me one night about a man that had come into the restaurant. As he was sitting there, she declared he was perfect for me and asked if I could come in immediately to meet him.

After definitively declining any interest in the prospect, I came in the next day to a note that said she had invited him to the restaurant to meet me at the end of my shift. He pulled up in front promptly at three, in a fancy, sporty, red vehicle with expensive rims. Though good-looking, he was completely self-involved and expected to eat for free. He definitely was not my type and possibly was an indication of what she thought of me (argh!), or an indication of why she didn't seem to have much luck in the man department herself.

I had known her for a year before we found a bit of common ground as we discovered there was a task we could work on together outside of the restaurant. Misha was a photographer and wanted to take my picture. I found that viewing myself through someone else's vision was quite enlightening to my self-discovery. As it turned out, all of her uncomfortable little quirks had a home in her amazing eye and quite innovative artistry of the absurd.

We spent the next two months speaking daily and working on a series of artistic fashion photos for my portfolio. During that time she met a man, and they became a fast couple. He was definitely not like the red-car guy but a serious, open-hearted, somewhat conservative business professional who really seemed to adore her in a way no one had. It changed her. The experience seemed to soften her jagged, quirky, uncomfortable-to-be-around, edges. Amazingly, her misery and loneliness seemed to disappear day by day. It was still winter (February, I think) when she and I finished the series of photos. After that she stopped communicating with me.

> The most impactful part of the experience to me today, is the gift of witnessing her actual process of ascension, the changes she made in her attitude and spirit created levity for her in many ways.

Ascension begins

I discovered that a few months before she ceased communication with me, she had also stopped connecting with other friends, including a woman with whom she was particularly close. All of us in her life were perplexed as it became a bit of happy-hour conversation. Within a few weeks, she'd given up her apartment, moved in with her lover, and planned to marry. If my memory serves me, I gave up the restaurant business for good around the same time, but still remained close with my friends there.

It was near the beginning of spring, the day had turned out to be just beautiful with the first scents of blooming flowers. I remember the the aroma in the air as I received the news. A call came into the restaurant. Misha drove a convertible SUV that had a soft top and a roll bar, which was a point of interest for me because the relaxed sportiness of the car never seemed to fit her exactly, and more notably, I always thought of it as such a dangerous vehicle to drive in the first place. Apparently, Misha had been driving on the I-10 freeway and had somehow lost control of her SUV and rolled. She was thrown from the vehicle and did not survive.

The epiphany

Shortly after the accident, while processing the initial loss, my relationship to Misha's broader life situation became clear. It was not the moment of impact and the way she died that was significant. It was the importance of those last few months and the way she lived. It was the transition from sadness into joy she took with her on that day.

The most meaningful part of the experience to me today, is the gift of witnessing her actual process of ascension, the changes she made in her attitude and spirit created levity for her in many ways, the same process I have witnessed in others who died from long-standing illnesses. Having already experienced a lot of loss in my life at that time, and not an average idea about death and dying from being psychic and empathic, I was in awe of being given the opportunity to be witness to this amazing process. It not only gave me hope and comfort about my own death and the eventual deaths of those close to me, it freed me from the illusion of death and gave me the opportunity to experience the kind of spiritual transition that is required from us when changing anything in our life be it large or small.

Death is the surrender to something more expansive than what you knew before.

> Love born of betrayal is better lost than lived.
>
> Higuemota Guevara

How I Met Higuemota

I have crossed the deep depression that Higuemota felt several times in my life. But none that compares to the depression that came after I had a late-term abortion when I was twenty-five and living in a five-floor walk-up, ghetto flat in New York City. It was a powerful time and those months being pregnant were the most transformational gift I could have been given. I'd never felt what it was like to have a foundation of peace. It was the opening of my clairvoyance and the expansion of my compassion into action. If I thought I had courage before, this new experience made me understand that my previous experiences were, maybe, brief moments of bravado.

This new wave of love and compassion I was experiencing was so protective and all-encompassing that I felt almost invincible. The interesting thing was that this feeling didn't include fantasy or the illusion of invincibility. There was such a peace about me that was centered in my own well-being—not that the world was well or that bad things don't happen, but that when they did happen, I'd be fine. Specifically, I remember thinking, *If all of the buildings come down around me, I'll be fine.*

During that time I crossed paths with the man who had mugged me a few months before. I followed him up the hill walking just feet behind him. During the mugging I hadn't been fearful, he'd had a knife and I gave up my money willingly. However, when he reached out to violate my body by touching my breast, I got tall. In that moment, I stood up very straight. I was not going to have any of it. I don't know what he saw, but I felt it. It was as if something was standing behind me or looking through my eyes.

He immediately said to the man with him, "Come on; let's go."

And, they were gone in a flash.

I suspected he was a local, but wasn't for sure until the day I followed him up the hill. As my gaze drilled into the back of his head, I knew he recognized me and yet he began to walk faster. I remember saying to him telepathically: *Oh, now you don't want to stop and chat, I see. It's a little different when you're by yourself.* By this time he was rounding the corner, and I needed to sit for a few moments and recover from the moment-to-moment exhaustion I was feeling because of the pregnancy.

As all of this was happening, I didn't know I was pregnant. In fact, I hadn't had a period for months and done several pregnancy tests that all came back negative. As it turned out, I conceived about four months into being treated for stress-related symptoms and never knew. All of the spiritual experiences that were happening seemed right in alignment with the changes I'd been making. And...I was sure I wasn't pregnant.

I INVEST MONEY IN CONDOMS AND I CHART MY FERTILITY LIKE AN EGYPTIAN ASTRONOMER TO AVOID PREGNANCY.

TRACY RENEE JONES

At that point in my life, I had no interest in having children. I understood that my burdens ran deep and didn't want to put them on anyone else, least of all on a child. I knew, on a core level, my life was about healing my spirit. Daily life in my apartment was a little rough. For at least six months, there'd been a main water pipe leak that had begun between the fourth and fifth floors.

I noticed when my kitchen ceiling fell in.

Water was gushing down. I ran upstairs to tell the guy above me about it, but when I walked into his kitchen, he also had no ceiling and a bucket perched on the edge of the counter capturing the water coming in...and he was frying some eggs. I couldn't believe it. How could he live like that? I suspected he wasn't in the country legally—he didn't speak English—and maybe he just didn't know what to do. I walked out, frustrated and shaking my head.

I called the city manager and in a few months they sent out a contractor. Evidently, getting a city bid was quite a task for a job this size. The building was more than 150 years old, and they were going to need to do a total re-pipe. Ron was the crew foreman, and he seemed to take quite a shine to me, but at the beginning I had no interest. He was twenty years older than me, and I didn't go for that kind of power struggle—at least that's how I saw it. (The truth was the man who'd raped me was also twenty years my senior.) Ron was an interesting man and quite charming. And he didn't approach me with definition. No, he subtly entered my spirit by always appearing at the right time, knowing things about me, and offering wisdom, a laugh, or a smile to plant seeds of his affection towards me. Honestly, beyond our attraction for each other, I didn't see him coming.

For about six months his consistent presence, charm, wit, and good looks wore me down...and he was single. He'd been asking me to dinner for months, but I always refused. Finally, I suggested one night that he come down to the jazz club where I worked, and we could go for a drink after. Something made me feel nervous, but I couldn't quite put my finger on it. I had already decided I wanted to have sex with him, so it wasn't about that. I wouldn't get pregnant, partly, I thought, because I hadn't had a period in a few months, but I always used condoms. I was sexually active in New York City in the eighties, and my momma didn't raise no fool. Although I'd always used multiple forms of birth control, this was the first month since I was eighteen that I'd had to go off birth-control pills. *That wasn't going to be a problem*, I thought. Again, I always used condoms.

Well, that special moment came and went. Yes, there was a condom mishap—or so he said—but it didn't make sense. I'd made sure he put it on, but somehow it ended up completely off.

To make matters worse, he went from being single, to being separated, to, "I'm leaving my wife for you because I love you...but I can't be seen with you in public." This all happened in about the span of two weeks' time. I understood that this wasn't the man for me. The job was done at my building and I stopped responding to his calls. I did see him around the neighborhood a few times, which was unexpected because he lived in Brooklyn. One day, I saw him again, driving near my house, which I thought was odd. He stopped, and as I was on my way to work, he asked me if I wanted a ride.

The only thing I remember from that conversation was the second thing out of his mouth. "Are you pregnant?"

Hmmm...that was an odd question, I thought. "No," I reassured him.

About two months later I was working at the restaurant one night when a lady sitting at table 20 exclaimed, "Are you pregnant!?"

"No, it's just the blouse I'm wearing."

"No," she said in a clear and concise tone. "You have a glow about you."

And then I knew. I *had* been feeling the glow. Everything began to make sense: the fatigue and different spiritual experiences. The pregnancy test I took that night was positive. The following day I was getting on a plane for a month-long journey in Arizona. What was I going to do?

Reproductive coercion

The next thirty days were painful on so many levels. At the time I'd been of the mindset that if I were ever to get pregnant, abortion would be an option. But now, the thought was just devastating. I wanted this baby, but I knew that everything surrounding it felt wrong. Every time I considered having it, I experienced an emotional pain like none before. After arriving in Arizona and visiting two different doctors, I now had my options.

I called Ron to discuss it. And what I heard on the other end of the line hit me like a torpedo. I couldn't speak. He told me that yes, he knew I was pregnant. He received it in a dream. He'd taken off the condom and intended to get me pregnant. He thought we'd have a very gifted child, he'd known it from the first day he saw me.

> His name was Dexter. He had so much love for his son and spoke about him all the time. I began to realize I knew more about Dexter than I did about his dad.

You see, it never occurred to me that a man would do that. You hear about women manipulating men to have babies all the time, but I'd never heard of a man manipulating or intimidating a woman into a pregnancy. As it turns out, today they have a name for it, when *anyone* does it. It's called *reproductive coercion*. Although it has not yet been criminalized here in the United States as it has in other countries, it is now being researched, acknowledged, and reported as intimate partner abuse.

I understood from my immense pain that there was no real decision to make, only acceptance of the circumstances and what I needed to do. I prayed to the spirit of my son. I told him that I could not bring him into a life like this, that while my circumstances would change, his father's nature wouldn't. I told the spirit of my son that I loved him deeply, and if he wanted to come back to me in another way at another time, that I would love to share a life with him. At that moment, the most powerful feeling of peace came over me, and I knew he understood.

The final detail to this story occurred approximately six years later in Los Angeles. I met a man, his name was Alan. We began to date, and while he was good to me, our relationship never quite clicked. He had a six-year-old son from his previous relationship he wanted me to meet. His name was Dexter. Alan had so much love for his son and spoke about him all the time. I began to realize I knew more about Dexter than I did about his dad. I knew all about his mom, when and where he was conceived, his ethnicity, what he liked and didn't like. Those thoughts began to wear on me. All the facts lined up to be very similar circumstances to my situation with Ron. My relationship with Alan wasn't working, but for some reason we held on. It would only be another week until his son came for a visit.

The day his son arrived with the nanny, the four of us went to dinner. The minute I saw this little boy my heart melted, and I began to tear up. I wondered why I was so emotional? Dex and I sat in the backseat, and Alan and the nanny were in the front seat, it felt as if they didn't exist. Dexter sat on my lap and hugged and kissed me as if we'd known each other for years. We laughed and played all the way through dinner and then on a trip to the grocery store. There was so much love between us it was surreal. Arriving at Alan's home, the nanny took the bags up stairs, but Dexter did not want to leave me. He stayed in a tight embrace as we hugged good-bye.

Finally, as it was getting late, Alan pulled him by the hand to leave and he fell to the ground, hanging on to my leg and screaming, "I want to stay with Mommy!"

I gasped, and my eyes welled up with tears. I knew who this young boy was. He is the young spirit who would have been my son, making sure I knew he'd made it in to this world okay. For Alan, however this was nothing but a six-year-old's tantrum. Nonetheless, they needed to get inside and settle down for the night, and I was going home. Alan pulled him away, and I blew a kiss and waved.

I never saw either of them again. I was filled with awe, love, peace, and gratitude for the gift of meeting him just one time.

The deliverance of Higuemota

One night I was in a bookstore that was going out of business. Everything was on sale. Something pulled me over to the poster section, and once again, I was caught breathless. In front of me was a poster of a midnight photograph of two dolphins swimming in the ocean under a quarter moon with an old, Spanish-looking pirate ship in the background. I stood there holding my heart as the tears and the vision started to come. A woman and her baby went overboard. I prayed to St. Michael to release them from their earthly bondage and deliver them back to the Creator.

Somehow all of the symbols in the photo were pertinent, but it was all too much to metabolize standing in the poster section of The Book Star at closing time. I snapped up the poster and headed to the counter. Even though I didn't know what all of this was, I knew it was going to be a lot of something, for which I had some trepidation. I did what I always do in this kind of a situation. I went home, hung the poster on the wall, and created an altar. I prayed for peace and strength through the unveiling of this story that I sensed had been held in my spirit for centuries.

The Slayer's Ritual: Are you ignoring something vital?

Answer these yes-or-no questions to get an idea of where you're at on the continuum of awareness.

- Do you feel a lot of anxiety? **Yes**___ **No**___
- Do specific situations trigger anxiety? **Yes**___ **No**___
- Do you find yourself noticing or paying a lot of attention to what others are doing or saying? **Yes**___ **No**___
- Do you find yourself being in judgment of others frequently? **Yes**___ **No**___
- Do you feel fearful more than half of the time about something? **Yes**___ **No**___
- Do you experience rejection more often than not in your life? **Yes**___ **No**___
- Does it seem that more than half of the situations you engage don't go your way? **Yes**___ **No**___
- Do you feel that things don't go your way because of others in your life? **Yes**___ **No**___
- Do you find yourself wanting or fantasizing about what other people have? **Yes**___ **No**___
- Does hearing the word *victim* elicit a feeling of comfort or anxiety? **Yes**___ **No**___

Results

0-3 Yes Answers: If you answered from zero to three questions yes, then you are self-aware and self-assured in general, but may find you are in the beginning of a new revolution of process regarding very specific subjects or dynamics. Pay attention to where and when you may have any feelings of self-consciousness or fear, for that is the indication that you are at the beginning of some new dynamic in yourself and your life.

3-6 Yes Answers: If you answered between three and six questions yes, then look alive. This is going to be an incredible new awakening for you in getting to know yourself. Pay attention to what you see, hear, and otherwise notice. The things that make you feel the most emotion are your guides in this phase of the spiritual process. Consider the things you notice the most, or that make you feel the most, are the things you are awakening to in yourself. This can be a very exciting and awe-inspiring part of the process if you remember that the fear and anxiety you feel are your friends and are the ways your spirit or unconscious self is communicating with your conscious mind. If the feelings ever get too intense, then remember breathing deeply from the diaphragm will help you to come back into your center and feel more relaxed.

6-10 Yes Answers: If you answered six or more questions with a yes, then instinct is your guide. The fight-or-flight response and the emotions that go with it will help you navigate this process. Any negative thoughts you have will be your biggest teachers. Remember, all negatives have positives at the other end of the spectrum. Consider that the positive side to your negative response is the message your higher self is seeking to get across to you.

The Slayer's Altar: I Have All I Need

Always, when creating a sacred space in your home, there is some sort of an impact. You'll get what you want, so it's important to completely understand what that means. If you're looking for peace in your life, then you've got to resolve the emotions that don't allow the space for peace, which might mean feeling sadness or grief for a period of time. Or, if you're looking for a new job or to lose weight, then the issue may have nothing to do with the donuts, but with other, less comfortable issues you need to think about. Either way there is a trade-off: letting go of one thing in order to create space for another.

Affirmation: I have all that I need at all times and am deeply appreciated for exactly who I am in this moment.

What you need:

- A clean and cleared space
- Black or purple jar candle
- The affirmation written on a piece of paper
- Glass of water

Place everything on the altar and light the candle for at least one hour a day. Keep a daily altar journal and document everything you think and feel as it relates to the affirmation. Daily, take time to notice what happens in your environment, what you watch on television, read in books or newspapers, and what you notice about other people whose paths you cross.

At the end of the altar, pour the water in your garden or down the toilet.

PART TWO

DON'T BE MAD

You've got the Upper Hand
No Matter what they Say

The Slayer's Weapons:

Confidence, Endurance, Self-Care, Responsibility, Trust

The Story of Xiao Xin

Xiao Xin was the daughter of the Chinese emperor Xian Feng. Her mother was Xian Feng's top concubine and his constant favoritism toward Xiao Xin created resentment within the family. Xian Feng and his family fled the Forbidden City at the end of the Second Opium War when Xiao Xin was four years old. The emperor died a year later. After that it was his closest confidant who took over the care of his favorite daughter as if she were his own.

Xiao Xin grew into a beautifully gentle young lady with a spirit of fire but her respect for tradition was worn out by the constant onslaught of resentment from her siblings. All Xiao Xin wanted was a life and family of her own without the politics and constant opinions and judgment of others.

Although she was betrothed to another, when she was sixteen Xiao Xin gave her heart and consequently her body to the love of her life, Cheng Li. This was the ultimate act of defiance against her family. He was an ambitious peasant man who dreamed of becoming a merchant to the world.

Xiao Xin always got what she wanted and what she wanted was Cheng Li. She knew that her time and secret was limited. Soon enough everything would be out in the open, and everyone would have to accept her choice. Little did she know that her mother already knew and had planned to kidnap Cheng Li, in order to send him on the next steamship to North America, thus saving her daughter the pain and humiliation of her actions.

The night was quite unseasonably warm as Xiao Xin made her way through a small section of forest to get to Cheng Li. The sound of the fallen leaves and twigs under her feet and the sweet fragrance of the Phoebe Zhennan trees weren't as calming as they had been all the other times she'd made the trip. Somehow this night was different. She was going to tell Cheng Li she was pregnant—maybe that was it.

The subtle aching in her stomach was unrelenting as she neared the end of the forest and Cheng Li's home came into view. Stopping abruptly and taking cover behind a Phoebe, she heard men speaking. Peering from behind the trunk, she saw her love unconscious and being held under each arm by two men that she recognized as her mother's guards. The pain from her stomach shot through the rest of her body and she began to bleed as she fell to her knees. What was happening to her? Her agony was palpable as she wailed and wept to the roots of that Phoebe. The last thing she heard the men say before she lost consciousness was *Strathairly.*

The cricket's song had given way to the less rhythmic chirping of the birds reflecting the sun's dawning. The birds were loud enough to wake her up, and it took her moments to remember where she was. She was completely out of sorts, dizzy and so heartbroken that she almost didn't notice she was bleeding. The blood coming from between her legs didn't compare to her fear and rage. She couldn't lose her love.

Xiao Xin came to understand about her mother's plan to put Cheng Li on the steamship Strathairly. Right now, she didn't care how her mother discovered their relationship or her condition; she needed to get to the Strathairly. She had to be on that ship with her love so she ran as fast as her feet would carry her.

> All Xiao Xin wanted was a life and family of her own without the politics and constant opinions and judgment of others.

The pain in her lower abdomen was numbed by the adrenaline that carried her across the forest floor, barely touching it, while the sun was slowly creeping up. Xiao Xin needed to be home in her quarters before it crossed the horizon. No one could know what she was doing. It would take at least two days' time to get to Shanghai and they were already several hours ahead of her. Clearly, there was no one she could trust.

Just before heading to her quarters, she tucked into a little room where they housed special herbs and medicines for everyday needs. She took what she could find, a few things to help with the cramping and any infection; she wasn't sure what was going on, but she suspected. Back in her quarters she wept as she cleaned herself up. She did not lose focus. Next, she sent a message to her mother saying that she had taken ill and did not want to be disturbed until she awoke on her own.

She threw a few pieces of clothing in a bag and pulled out a wooden box Cheng Li had given her. In it was some money and a hairpin that only married ladies wore. It was a symbol of their sacred union. She wrapped her long, pitch-black locks into a bun and secured them triumphantly with the hairpin. She put on a garment that was beneath her status and headed out to the stables, where the stable boy was making a complicated repair. She got on her mother's favorite stallion and, completely undetected, off she rode to her love.

In hindsight the journey almost seemed impossible, considering all that had happened. She arrived in one and a half days' time, still fueled by adrenaline, hungry, tired, and betrayed. She searched for the *Strathairly*, but it was nowhere to be found. Had she gotten the name wrong? Had it already left? She found the next steamship leaving port, the *Suez*, and found a way to get on it. The ride, the miscarriage, the betrayal, all seemed to be catching up to her as the *Suez* pulled out to sea.

"Was this the right thing to do?" Xiao Xin asked herself. The money from the box didn't seem to be going as far as she'd thought. The voyage was rumored to last up to forty days' time, and she had not lost count. It was day thirty-eight. The people on this ship were not what she was used to, and somehow she got lost in the mix of all the activity and anticipation of the arrival on American soil. Everyone seemed so desperate; she tried to keep her distance the best she could.

Disembarking was extremely chaotic in Seattle. She roamed the port looking for the steamship *Strathairly*.

She asked the first man she saw, "Do you know if the *Strathairly* has come into port?"

"It arrived two days ago," he said.

He was an odd-looking man: short and slight with a wiry frame. At first appearance he seemed quite old. But as Xiao Xin looked closer, he wasn't old at all. His face was deeply scarred, from what she couldn't tell. He seemed to have kind eyes, and until two days ago she'd been able to trust everyone. People called him Benny.

"Are you looking for someone who arrived on the *Strathairly*?"

"My husband," she replied.

"Well there is an eatery about a mile down the road where almost everyone goes to look for work. I can take you there if you like. You must be hungry."

"That would be kind of you," she said.

Those words would soon become her biggest regret. Little did she know that Benny was a well-known Crimp down on the docks who made his money from trickery whether it was selling women to sailors or selling sailors to the big ship bosses who never seemed to have enough hands on deck. Benny had been a fixture along the West Coast for the last ten years and was known for being a fairly ruthless businessman.

The thick, oily pockmarked skin of his face took all of the attention from his hazel eyes and the long mustache. It was certain to have been the cause of much ridicule for it wasn't easily overlooked. Always dressed in overalls and a suit jacket, he blended in and would lurk about undetected like a cobra waiting to strike. The black clouds were beginning to roll in with some lightening absent of thunder, just the chilling silence of the clouds rolling in with the whispering winds of change.

Strolling down the road a piece to the eatery, they overcame the silence with some uncomfortable chatter. Xiao Xin was beginning to feel nervous and unwell. The ocean journey had really taken its toll; she was lucky that she hadn't gotten an infection from the miscarriage. She had to find Cheng Li but he was not at the eatery.

"Sit down, honey, I'll treat you to a hot meal," said Benny. "And don't worry, I'm sure he will show up."

Now only feeling her nerves, a little relief came when he ordered her some soup and a cup of hot tea and then suggested she take a trip to the ladies' room to get herself cleaned up before the order arrived.

Benny had never offered food to one of the girls before, but somehow this one was different. He was a little taken by her beauty and grace. Benny wanted this one for himself.

Xiao Xin woke up in a cage and was filled with panic and confusion. The man had dosed her with some opium and brought her home to his dirty flat on the south side of Seattle. She began to scream and cry. She wailed until her throat hurt and then fell asleep on the thin blanket he'd left in the cage for her.

Some hours later he arrived back at the flat. She had no concept of the time; all she knew was that it was dark, cold, and silent. Benny entered the room and pulled a chair up next to the cage.

"Look, honey, you seem like a sweet girl. I like you. I can tell you're real smart because your English is good. So listen up: as long as you do what I want when I want, I'll let you out of this thing…but if you disobey me or try to run I will leave you in here forever."

It would be a six-year journey of fear being turned into courage, every day waiting and believing that her beloved Cheng Li was out there and that she would find him.

Thus began the battle of wills. It would take Benny months of rapes, beatings, and long, cold nights in the cage to finally get her to submit. For Xiao Xin it would be a six-year journey of fear being turned into courage, every day waiting and believing that her beloved Cheng Li was out there, and that she would find him.

As the story went, Benny loved Xiao Xin as much as he could love at all and had begun to give her some freedom. Although he never shared her with anyone, he would threaten to do so, just to keep her in line. One day while out at the open market, it finally happened—she saw Cheng Li. They both had changed so much, but she knew in her heart it was him. Swiftly, she walked over, making believe that she twisted her ankle right in front of him.

As he knelt down to help her, she said, "Cheng Li, it is me, Xiao Xin. Please, don't speak, I am in danger, and we must be discreet."

Cheng Li's eyes filled with tears, he recognized that voice. There were too many feelings to communicate in that moment, so instead he looked at her and listened.

"I am being held captive by a very powerful man. Benny has eyes everywhere. We must make a plan and execute it perfectly."

She stopped for a moment, not having considered if Cheng Li had married and moved on, and in that moment she knew he could never love another as he loves her.

"Do you still love me?" she asked.

"Yes," Cheng Li whispered, tears falling from his eyes.

"Help me up like a gentleman and meet me back here next week at the same time," she said.

"I will be here," he promised as he helped her up. As she walked away he said, "Good day, Madame."

It had been a hard, long winter for both of them. Cheng Li had since moved to a fairly new mining town, Jerome, Arizona. Even with snow on the ground it felt warm compared to Seattle. Commerce was building there and Cheng Li had somehow steered clear of all the lecherous people and made a place for himself selling goods and handyman services at a little storefront next to the brothel. He was in good favor with many influential people, and of course all the girls next door loved the gentleness in his eyes.

Cheng Li would travel to Seattle every three months to purchase sweets, spices, and other goods for his store. The trip to Jerome took a little over a week and he couldn't afford to miss the appointed day and time to meet his love, he would need to find a place to stay. His next stop was his spice supplier. Although he didn't know him well he trusted him; they were from the same village in China. Surely he would know who this Benny was and what to do.

It would take a year of meeting and strategizing from that point to execute their plan perfectly. It was the spring of Xiao Xin's sixth year in captivity when she left Benny's dirty flat for the last time. She walked peacefully to the market, ducking in through the spice shack and out a back door into a carriage waiting for her. Cheng Li was anxiously waiting in Jerome for his beloved. Now it would only be days.

You've never seen two people seize every moment that they had together in harmony. Their love was invincible and miraculous, healing all of the pain, hardship, and betrayal that had befallen their lives and yet prospering them into goodness. Cheng Li's business was thriving and soon he taught Xiao Xin so that she could take care of things when he traveled. They spent long nights talking and expelling their grief and sorrows of the past. Cheng Li held his heart when she told him of their unborn child and the loss that night. Xiao Xin also asked his forgiveness for the way her family had betrayed them both.

Finally Cheng Li spoke: "We knew our path was not an easy one; neither of us lied to ourselves. We made it through. You are my deepest beloved, Xiao Xin; do not sorrow any further for our unborn son, for we will create another."

Xiao Xin fell into his arms weeping lightly and make another they did. The years of contentment went by, both of them deeply imbibing their mundane day-to-day life adventures. Their beautiful boy, Shen Woo, was just turning five when the flu hit the town. Xiao Xin knew that this was the beginning of the end.

Benny, meanwhile, had turned into an absolute madman. He'd not known anything but control in his life and wasn't able to surrender to his extraordinary loss. Everyone kept their distance from him as best they could for he was on the verge of evil. He had spent the last six years looking for Xiao Xin and plotting to bring her back, conjuring all the ways he would make her suffer. Xiao Xin could feel him coming. The six months following Shen Woo's death from the flu, Xiao Xin couldn't speak and could barely get out of bed. Cheng Li was doing his best to keep things going, but even he felt the end coming.

It was a dark night with no moon, and the air was still and pungent with the smell of sage. Benny had been having them watched for months and would now take his revenge. He had rented a room just outside of the community, near a secondary mine in the town; he had even brought the cage for effect. He slipped quietly into the store and up the stairs to their bedroom. Cheng Li was asleep, but Xiao Xin hadn't been able to close an eye.

Benny pulled Cheng Li out of the bed and slit his throat before she could scream. He wanted her to see his greasy pockmarked face and the green of his eyes while he witnessed her terror. Benny then dragged her out of the bed by her hair and in one fell swoop cut off her long, rich black locks into a jagged horror. Stripping her of her clothing and wrapping her motionless body in a blanket, he carried her out where his men were waiting to take them down the mountain to the den of hell that he had created just for her. She remained numb and motionless.

> Their love was invincible and miraculous, healing all of the pain, hardship, and betrayal that had befallen their lives and yet prospering them into goodness.

He violently threw her in the cage, beating her across the head a couple of times and taking the blanket. Again he pulled up the chair beside her, but this time he called in his men. Soon there were at least ten others in the room, all drunk and jeering at her. She quietly placed her hand over her vagina, not that it mattered, but it made her feel better. After about thirty minutes, he dismissed the men to continue their drinking in the other room. Benny got up from the chair and in the gas light Xiao Xin saw a flash. It was the blade of a knife attached to the back of his belt; she'd never noticed it before. He walked to the cabinet and pulled out a lady's slip that clung to the body and didn't cover much.

"Put this on so that you can look like the whore you are," said Benny. "I gave you everything and treated you like a queen, and you do this to me? First, I am going to do things to you you've never heard of, and then I am going to let every man out there have an hour with you. How does that sound?"

After Xiao Xin put on the slip, the high pitch of the slowly moving, creaking cage door filled her with an awareness she'd not experienced before. For the first time in months she felt awake and alert. She had no sorrow, no pain, no fear, just clarity and fortitude.

Benny pulled her out of the cage by her hair and threw her to the floor. She grappled at his feet to get her bearings, and then grabbing at his pants, one hand holding onto the suspender and the other unzipping the fly, she said, "Benny, please let me make it up to you."

Groveling would buy her some time so that she could gain the proper footing. Now she had both feet on the ground, unhooking his suspenders. Grabbing the knife as his pants fell to the ground, she plunged the knife directly into his heart. He let out a loud yelp and struggled to get the knife out of her grip. Hearing the commotion, one of his men ran into the room. Assessing what happened, he shot her on sight.

One thing is for certain: they all will eventually get their love back.

The Slayer's Path: Stay in the Game

The devil looks for every opportunity to lead you astray or get you to quit. Demons will do anything to lead you away from the things and people that will lead you away from them. They want you to believe they're always in control and will use manipulation, fear, and intimidation in order to keep you physically, emotionally, mentally, or spiritually hostage to their whims.

The natural response to feeling trapped is the desire to escape, to run from the situation. The truth is, the most powerful position is to stay intact and involved in the event. When you stay put, you have the opportunity to assess the circumstances and then make a decision that can offer relief. Staying in the situation doesn't necessarily mean staying in the physical situation, especially if you're in danger. But sometimes it does. When you stay physically connected to an event, you call all of your power to that time and place, making you empowered to make a difference. No matter how undesirable, uncomfortable, or scary a situation feels to you, believe it or not you are stronger staying put than you are running.

The devil and reality

Reality is the result that occurs from your choices and actions. The devil can't hurt you: The devil gets you to hurt yourself. Whenever you hear the awful news stories of someone saying that God or the devil told them to do it, maybe it's true, but the person (not God or the devil) was the one who made the choice to do it.

The Slayer's Path: **Stay in the Game**

When any influence wants to get you to hurt yourself or someone else, it's wrong. It boils down to your own integrity. How much faith do you have in the possibility of refusing to hurt yourself or others, even in the direst of situations? Let me just throw into the mix here that refusing to hurt someone else doesn't mean sacrificing yourself either. It is possible for you to make the choice not to be hurt or to hurt anyone else.

> The first thing to do when in a dangerous situation is avert any detrimental crisis by calling in help.

The Slayer's Motto: Not an Option

The slayer's motto can be used in any context that involves behavior or choices, thoughts or feelings. Feeling disrespected is a common reason people engage in conflict. Now, whether or not a person is actually disrespected is not the point. And, at the end of the day, it doesn't really matter. It is the *perception* of disrespect and the hurt feelings that come with it that creates a space for confusion and conflict.

For example, every time I get in the car I say to myself, *Getting into any sort of accident is not an option.* It sets a natural, energetic boundary that aligns me with the *not getting into any sort of accident* vibe and opens up the energetic opportunities to get where I am going safely. This claim works well in any crisis or dangerous situation; it not only helps you override any fear you may have but also illuminates the explicit process of how things occur.

When you align every part of your energy towards the same goal, you can actually mobilize the molecules around you to create a protective barrier in times of trouble. While we don't yet have scientific proof of this universal fact, it certainly can't hurt to get used to the concept. Now, make no mistake about it: it's not a remedy for doing something stupid like standing in the middle of the train tracks waiting for the oncoming train because you want to see if you can move it with your mind. Chances are, your bodiless spirit will end up saying, *Oops! That's not what I meant.*

MAY THE ROAD RISE TO MEET YOU. MAY THE WIND ALWAYS BE AT YOUR BACK. MAY THE SUN SHINE WARM UPON YOUR FACE AND RAINS FALL SOFT UPON YOUR FIELDS. AND UNTIL WE MEET AGAIN, MAY GOD HOLD YOU IN THE PALM OF HIS HAND.

IRISH PROVERB

Learning to handle anger, fear, anxiety, and grief

Some of the most debilitating emotions we feel are anger, fear, grief, and anxiety; they can stop us dead in our tracks. At times they leave us paralyzed, put us in a rage, or lead us to an ill-considered response. Being able to remain yourself in a time of crisis is paramount not only to disarming otherworldly influences but to change the entire outcome of a situation.

Call for help

There is no shame in asking for help. If you are in a physically or emotionally dangerous situation, which means you are going to hurt yourself or someone else, the first thing to do is call for help. This may mean calling a friend or neighbor or 911 if necessary. Make sure your physical world is secure first.

Next, if you are witnessing someone (or yourself) have an emotional upheaval or spiritual battle, then say a prayer to call in your higher self or the archangels for assistance. If you are a person who carries any of these emotions, then you know how quickly it can come on, overwhelming you or the situation you find yourself in. When you are in a time of peace, take time to consider what you would do in a dangerous situation, whether the danger be physical, emotional, mental, or spiritual.

I received a communication one night from a friend who'd been called into a situation that quickly became debilitating. She was at her friend Jeremy's house and he was in a drug-exacerbated crisis. Jeremy was raging, grieving, and cutting himself. When she arrived he was fully clothed in the bathtub bleeding from a few places. She was able to calm him down and tend to his cuts. But what made her reach out to me was what he was saying. He was going back and forth from hateful, vulgar language to deeply self-pitying rants, both indications of demonic influence, which is common with drug users. Eventually she talked him into going to the hospital where he stayed a few nights, and from there he went to drug rehab.

> Everything makes a sound if you are tuned in, even spirits. Breathe. Bring your awareness to your ears…now listen.

Stop, look, and listen

Are you always aware of yourself and your surroundings? Well, the next step is to learn and practice becoming aware with *stop, look, and listen.* Stop what you are doing and slow your breath—breathe deeply. Become aware of your adrenaline and its flow through your body and slow it, bringing your awareness to your eyes. Breathe.

Look around yourself for information. What's happening? Is there movement? Sound? Are you indoors or out? Is it day or night? Are there others? Who or what are they? Real or spiritual? Yes, this is the time to train yourself to become aware on all levels of your surroundings.

Listen. Everything makes a sound if you are tuned in, even spirits. Breathe. Bring your awareness to your ears. Name five things you hear and write them down.

At some point during your day, stop, look, and listen. Over time you will train your subtle awareness.

> Take time to consider, when you are in a time of peace, what you would do in a dangerous situation, whether the danger be physical, emotional, mental, or spiritual.

Decide what's not an option

You have the power and jurisdiction to decide what will or won't be an option in any situation. Here is a new philosophy: *if you're there, you own it.* This means that whatever is going on around you includes you in some way. You have a part in it on some level, which means you also have power in it on some level as well. There are no coincidences; your presence has meaning, power, and influence on the situation you find yourself in. Now that you know you are empowered, decide what cannot be an option in your situation. My friend choose, while on the drive to Jeremy's house, that death or further violence was not an option.

Decide the outcome in advance

Yes, you can decide the outcome of a situation in advance. This comes down to the basic principal of magic: be clear on your intention. If you are in a crisis situation and have the presence of mind to decide the outcome, that's power.

> At the beginning, when a person is victimized, the very experience of victimization implies a lack of awareness. How can you keep something from happening when you don't know it exists? When a person is victimized it is not their fault. It is the perpetrator's fault. Period.

Decide no one can be hurt

When you decide on all levels that no one will be hurt in any circumstance, you energetically open up the door to many other possibilities that don't include people getting hurt. It really is that simple.

I lived in New York City's Harlem in the mid-1980s. It was a bit rough and tumble at that time, and late one summer evening I was leaving to go to the jazz club where I worked around ten p.m. with my good friend Sara. She'd stopped by to pick me up and had gotten out of the car to ring the buzzer. I came down and just as we walked to the car I saw a young man in a blue hoodie. He was rounding the corner and briskly making his way towards us. I completely tuned out Sara, and put my complete attention on him. We made eye contact, and I knew he was up to no good. Everything about his gait, focus, and gaze told me so.

I kept my eyes fixed on him and said to him in my mind, *I am not the one for you tonight. I am not the one.*

When he got to within 10 feet of us, he quickly moved to the driver's side, grabbed Sara, put a knife to her rib cage, and said, "Give me your purse."

She did, and he was gone. Sara and I stood there stunned. I even think we laughed a bit. To keep this all in perspective, the entire event happened in less than a minute. Yes, a New York City minute.

I learned quite a bit from that experience. Afterwards, I spent a lot of time feeling guilty, pondering why I couldn't or didn't protect her too. However, the answer that always came was, *What happened, was in fact, the highest possibility.* In hindsight, there really wasn't enough time to alert her in advance; and who knows, maybe she would have been hurt if I'd tried to warn her. Personally, I was hyper-vigilant and had spent quite a bit of time committing to myself that I would never be hurt again. I was aware of him and had previously spent time making my decision about the outcome. Essentially, I had excluded myself. Her focused awareness on other things at the time of the event made her energetically available in the situation.

The Slayer's Motto: **Not an Option**

Please don't misconstrue what I'm saying here. This is one of those new age concepts that needs to be fully explained to be understood. There is no blame on Sara; it wasn't her fault, and she did not deserve it. When a person is victimized, the very experience of victimization implies a lack of awareness. How can you keep something from happening when you don't know it exists? When a person is victimized, it is not their fault. It is the perpetrator's fault. Period.

Now, what happens to the victim is that they begin down the path of an emotional and spiritual journey that helps them to better understand the process of the Universe, and the path to understanding that reveals forethought and foresight. The reality is that once you've been victimized, your journey of self-loathing, shame, and guilt become the teachers of your understanding, your personal spiritual patterns, and the process by which you become self aware.

Decide to be effective or walk away

Doing demon battle is a power struggle in its simplest form, and probably the most important lesson for a slayer is to know when they can't win the battle and must walk away. I didn't understand this fully, although I'd had multiple experiences of it in my life. How I always couched it was, *You've got to know your limits,* and in fact you do. But, that's not quite what I'm talking about here.

In our world there are killers and criminals who are single-minded, lack empathy, and are often supported with demonic energies. Pitting your force against their force, directly, is not wise. I was really struck and troubled when the Columbine school shooting happened. For an empath, events like that are tumultuous. I grieved for days, for all of them. What I didn't quite understand was the force I felt from and around Eric Harris and Dylan Klebold, the killers. It most certainly was connected to something otherworldly, but what I really couldn't connect to was the denseness of the boy's energy. As an empath, I can usually connect at will to just about anyone, energetically. But this time I could not, they had no doors or windows open to my vibration. I asked to receive a dream to help me better understand them. It was Nguvu Jabari who replied.

"Do not enter a battle you cannot win. Do not stand against a force you cannot overcome. Stand back or be absent, and prepare for another way."

Learning to Trust Your Gut is Key

What's in a name?

Every time I came home from school telling Mom about the new boy I met, her first question would be, "What's his last name?"

The first time I was a bit perplexed. *Hmmm, why is this so important?* I eventually learned that it is always important to know who you're dealing with and what's in your environment—the more information the better. When a person states his full name, not only does the name itself have meaning, but a person's essence is revealed in their voice. I can hear a bit about their nature and frame of reference, the lens through which they look at life. Mom always said that a boy who won't tell you his whole name is not worth knowing, and that has proven to be true.

For a brief time I had a neighbor, Michelle, who I was chummy with. She came home one evening very excited about this new guy she'd met at the bus stop. It made me laugh that the automatic question I had for her was, "What's his last name?"

She responded, "I don't know."

I was just as perplexed as the day my mom asked me that question. Why would a grown woman (she was in her thirties) accept a date with a man and not know his full name?

She came over to borrow some jewelry, and as she was trying on some options to wear on her date, we chatted. In a joking manner, I asked, "How are you going out with a guy when you don't know his last name?"

She laughed and said, "That doesn't matter, he is fine."

"Did you get a business card?"

"No," she said. "Why are you asking me all of this—wait, do you know something?"

"I don't think so…"

But why was I so focused on this? It was food for thought. She chose a pair of earrings and my favorite vintage glass bead necklace and was on her way to meet him at a blues club downtown.

The next morning around seven Michelle called. She was crying and frantic. The man she'd been out with had kidnapped and raped her. After he fell asleep she was able to escape and run for her life, making it out of the nasty motel room he'd taken her to, with only her purse, shirt, and pants—no shoes and no jewelry.

We spent the next five hours at the rape crisis center. I was her support system as she didn't have any friends or family in town. She endured the rape kit and the regurgitation of her story to the rape crisis staff and the detectives. She was devastated and in shock. Finally, late that afternoon I delivered her to her door, in hopes she would have a good night's sleep. It was now about thirty-six hours without sleep for Michelle, and tomorrow we had a date with the detectives.

Luckily, the man who raped her wasn't a very good criminal. He actually lived at the fleabag motel where he raped her, had prior convictions, and took her phone call. At the suggestion of the detectives we used my left-behind jewelry as bait and he agreed to a meeting to return it. The police picked him up, and he's now serving time in jail for his crimes.

Michelle will also be living with his crimes for years to come, I imagine. While it is possible to recover completely and fully from the trauma and damage that rape creates, it's a long haul. And it can take years of personal work to restore yourself from such a detriment. Michelle and I lost touch a few months later when she went back to her hometown. I know that for some victims of violent crime, it's easier to move through what happened by letting go of all who were present in their lives at the time of the event. I think of her often and pray for her peace, and I am honored to have donated my jewelry to such an important cause.

> IF EQUALLY MATCHED, WE CAN OFFER BATTLE; IF SLIGHTLY INFERIOR IN NUMBERS, WE CAN AVOID THE ENEMY; IF QUITE UNEQUAL IN EVERY WAY, WE CAN FLEE FROM HIM.
>
> SUN TZU

Resistance

Once you've made up your mind about how you need things to be and have begun to cultivate a slayer's awareness of yourself and your environment, the next thing is to understand the spiritual process of that awareness and ultimately the spiritual process of change.

Resistance is the phase of spiritual process where the evidence of the change is connecting to our conscious mind through extreme negativity or resistance. You know you are resisting when you use phrases like *I'd never do that* or *That person is so rude.* Whatever you are acknowledging through a negative perspective is either the change that is beginning in your life or what you yourself are already doing.

They have a saying in the recovery community: "You spot it, you got it."

Resistance is a wonderful place to be. It proves that you are one step before the breakthrough that you are seeking. It is a fundamental part of the spiritual process of becoming. This kind of resistance does not mean you are not receptive to what you want, only that you are pushing against the obstacle in its way. It's like doing resistance training with weights. You add extra pressure against your muscles so that they work harder to break the old pattern of movement. The energy of resistance hits the strongest point just before the breakthrough or realization. Resistance plays a fundamental role in the process of transition: when you ask for change it is because you are ready on some level to begin the conscious process to receive that change.

Thinking negatively is a part of our spiritual process and the way our higher spiritual consciousness enters into the emotional body to become a part of our physical world experience.

What is a breakthrough?

A breakthrough is the point at which the unconscious mind brings to the conscious mind the presence of the goal and any obstacles to it. Until this point, the conscious mind has been unaware of why it doesn't have what it says it wants or is unclear about what it wants altogether. Resistance is by far the easiest to spot in someone else, and if you are moderately self-aware, then it sticks out like a sore thumb when you experience it. This is where we get into the power of negative thinking. Yes, that's right: the power of negative thinking. Being able to understand the message from spirit, through your negative thoughts, is the key.

> Change does not happen overnight.

Get on board with your shadow

For years, all the buzz has been about positive thinking, and don't get me wrong: for those who can do it truthfully, it's nothing to snub your nose at. Have you ever found yourself getting irritable with a friend, making every effort to think positively about something that, no matter how you slice it—it's just not good? If you've ever lost a loved one, the worst thing anyone can say to you in consolation is, *Well, they lived a good life*, or *They're in a better place*. You know when facing the death of someone close to you, that none of those seemingly kind words help your loss or grief in any way, and those who've been in your shoes would never say them.

Thinking negatively is a part of our spiritual process and the way our higher spiritual consciousness enters into the emotional body to become a part of our physical world experience. Our negative thinking has been called many things over the years; it has been called our duality, darkness, bad side, shadow, or evil just to name a few. Its energy is dense, and the language we use to describe it is potent and penetrating. A harsh word from a friend can be like a dagger to the heart.

Negative thinking is an intrinsic part of the way we are able to process information from spirit to the brain and body through our emotion, and often it can incite self-consciousness, shame, or pain we've taught ourselves to avoid at all costs. It is my experience that whatever you reject vehemently boomerangs back to you until it is resolved peacefully. The idea here is not to judge ourselves, but to accept ourselves so fully that we embrace our negative thoughts as evidence of breakthroughs to come. To understand what's on its way, we learn to interpret our negative thoughts as their polar opposites would imply. The higher self speaks to us through our awareness, and sometimes we are only able to recognize the messages from the density of the emotion or thought forms we experience. Essentially, a negative thought has a positive meaning.

Change does not happen overnight. As we all know, there is a process to letting go, and many stages to feeling as we begin to be more comfortable without the object of our loss. There is also a process to receiving: otherwise we'd perceive we have all we want all the time, and what fun would that be? Acknowledging resistance and the presence of your shadow is embracing the inevitable change.

How do you know if you're in resistance?

It is my experience we all are in transition with something most of the time. You may find you answered these questions *yes* in relation to certain aspects of your life but not others. Pay attention to the themes that come up as you consider each one, like taking notice of what emotional circumstances make you feel physical pain, or want to sleep in response. For those of you who answered all of the questions *no*, Woo Whoo! You have found surrender.

- Do you have difficulty seeing the cup half full? **Yes**___ **No**___
- Are your emotional reactions above and beyond what the situation calls for? **Yes**___ **No**___
- Do you frequently use words like "never" or "always"? **Yes**___ **No**___
- Do you find yourself being offended or using sarcasm frequently? **Yes**___ **No**___

- At times, do you find that you have a sensation of physical pain that accompanies an emotional response? **Yes___ No___**
- Do you want to sleep as a response to strong emotional reaction? **Yes___ No___**
- Do friends or family tell you that you have selective hearing? **Yes___ No___**
- Do you often spend time wondering why things happen to you? **Yes___ No___**

> Negative thinking is an intrinsic part of the way we are able to process information from spirit to the brain and body through our emotion.

The Slayer's Pact: Respect your Elders

Recognizing the contributions of your ancestors is the true meaning of respecting your elders. Every generation is born with certain attributes that allow its members the ability to accomplish certain tasks for the evolution of humanity. And every generation that is born must work to understand those that came before and those who will come after. It makes sense that the people born to create the industrial age would be practical-minded and lack empathy to a certain degree, but then give birth to an entire generation where sexual, emotional, and ideological freedoms are the focus.

On an interpersonal level, respecting your parents is the action of compassion and love for all they have sacrificed so that you can be here. It's not a free pass if you were abandoned or abused by them, or if they behaved badly. It's about choosing not to be mad and to take care of yourself when and where they left off. Sometimes people who have lived longer than you just may have more information about many things to which you now have access through them—if you can let go of feeling judged by them.

How I Met Xiao Xin

The steady crackle of my slow moving truck driving down the gravel road was somehow invigorating to me. The noon sun was hot and high, and its glare reflected into my eyes causing me to drive so slowly. The rich smell of wild sage and lavender in the summer heat was all encompassing, so much so that I didn't notice my right foot slowing the truck to a complete stop at the bottom of the gully.

A huge desert tarantula appeared about twenty feet in front of me in the middle of the road. I saw the movement of the little creature going as fast as it could to cross. I was overcome with tears to be honored with such a sighting and for that moment, sitting in the sacred center of the world and having access to all things. On the path of spiritual awareness there comes a time when all dimensions become obvious, when the unresolved past is the present and obscures the future until you sit for a moment viewing all four directions from the sacred center. I must have sat there in contemplation for at least ten minutes watching the lady spider get to her destination, until I heard the sound of a vehicle crackling up the road behind me.

The Slayer's Pact: **Respect Your Elders**

Sedona, Arizona, is the Mecca of the West. Spiritualists travel far and wide to experience the amazing, energetic vortices that are revered to hold the spiritual matrix of the planet. I have journeyed there several times and have never been disappointed in the experience.

On the route I take, the road goes through a quaint little town of about 444 people called Jerome. It is an old-west mining town that experienced its American heyday in the late 1800s, known for its gold, copper, and silver mines, and of course the history of its many whorehouses. The archives are rich with fast-made money, bigotry, addiction, and abuse. Being an empath, the first time I went was overwhelming. The density of the dark spiritual residue left behind from the corruption was profound. I am certain it attracted all kinds; I could feel it. The vibe smacked of serial killer.

Over many visits and many years, the folks who lived there and the folks who passed through began to change. The denseness of the spirit there was being whittled away by the loving intent to transform its pain into creation, and soon it became a vibrant creative center where the energy was inspiring. I'd found a house there, nestled in the mountain almost all the way to the top. The views were spectacular and unencumbered. I had driven up with a friend who was into real estate *and* ghostbusting, so it was a win-win.

Arriving at the Grand Hotel—famous for being an insane asylum for the first half of its life until a couple of guys came in and made the old, abandoned building a hotel (they cleverly sported a fine dining restaurant called The Asylum)—we found the lobby clean and moderately restored, but it still smelled old, while the rooms hadn't been refurbished since the 1980s.

The view, however, was amazing, as the ol' girl sat at the highest point of town and looked out over the entire Verde Valley and the beautiful red rocks of Sedona. We checked into our room, dropped our bags, and headed out for some ghost hunting. What we found instead was some wine, a local psychic, and a lovely sunset. After dinner at The Asylum, we went up to the room to gather Janice's ghostbusting equipment. There were definitely ghosts to be discovered. Much to our dismay, none of the equipment worked. It just simply did not work; the freshly charged batteries had all gone dead. It was late. We laughed and went to bed.

The night was just beginning for me. Our small stale room with a view had a very old queen bed with a twin bed only a few feet away. The outer linens felt dusty, but the sheets seemed to be fine. I fell fast asleep and was lying on my back with my legs splayed out when I began to have a dream of a sexual nature. I felt a wet tongue all over my privates, and I became breathless. It wasn't until the heat of my body along with a subtle gasp for air made me realize that it wasn't really happening, even though it felt so real.

This wasn't a dream. I was fully aware and the sensation was still happening. I opened my eyes and there was Xiao Xin. She propped herself up onto her knees and looked at me smiling and covering her mouth with her right hand, letting out a little giggle. As she stood at the end of the bed, I looked deeply at her small, slight frame, the fragility and strength in her eyes, the short blunt black hair, the crimson red slip, her red lips, and a long set of pearls she was wearing around her neck. In the moments before she dissipated, I knew that she was me. I just knew and I wept. I looked over and Janice was fast asleep.

> On the path of spiritual awareness there comes a time when all dimensions become obvious, when unresolved past is the present and obscures the future until you sit for a moment viewing all four directions from the sacred center.

In the weeks after that experience, Xiao Xin began to tell me her story. It made my pain finally make sense, at least some of it anyway. I grieved for her and for me for days. Finally, I was able to free that part of my spirit and let her rejoin her origins in the oversoul.

The Sacred Center

Being human is pretty spectacular on every level, but being able to create another life form with our essence is amazing. Whether or not you want or have children is not the point. Our bodies are a sacred ground where our heart, mind, and spirit can flourish or wither. This space can be a life-generating microcosm that gives us access to all that is, or it can be a storage unit for all the pain and suffering we've ever had. It all depends on how we see things. Becoming aware of our vast, human ability to heal ourselves and the Earth by connecting through our sacred center is a profound rite of passage.

The sacred center is the area of your body from your navel to the end of your pelvic bone and the perceived round space that encompasses all sides of this part of the body. It is the place where we can generate new life on all levels, connect, ground, and heal ourselves. It is our anchoring power center where we carry a reservoir of cosmic life force that generates the *kundalini* energy in the body. This life force is sometimes called the prenatal life force, which creates the understanding that some people are born with it already cultivated and others will cultivate it in their lifetime.

Prana, chi/qi, and kundalini are all names for this unifying life force that connects our body, mind, and spirit and the sacred center is its home. Have you ever heard of someone referred to as having a *strong constitution*? No matter what they eat or drink or do, they never seem to get sick. Well, they have a strong, cultivated life force reservoir. Often, people who come in with a cultivated life force have problems feeling or controlling their anger when they enter puberty. They have an abundance of life force, but no developed direction for it.

Benny, from the Xiao Xin parable, is an example of cultivated life force, as is Xiao Xin. Puberty is traditionally the time of the first kundalini awakening we experience, although forms of trauma can bring about an awakening prematurely. Each of the glands that make up our endocrine system can be awakened by the kundalini energy.

The Slayer's Ritual: Becoming Aware of Your Sacred Center

The sole purpose for doing ritual is to create a discipline for inner and outer awareness. The more awareness you have, the more peaceful you become. Your ritual then becomes the expression of your commitment to your goal. Discipline is something that is developed over time, and everyone will begin this process with a different level of discipline. The exercise I have created is designed to give you the full experience of the before, during, and after of engaging in ritual and to amplify your attention to your inner voice.

Having said that, in my life there have been times of great duress when I surely would have gone running from such a tedious set of instructions. So please understand that anything you do is better than doing nothing. You can do no wrong when it comes to ritual, and there are times when simple is best, and only you truly know what is best for you. Below is a template that—once you have gone through it in its entirety—you can then modify and make your own.

Fifteen minute awareness session

Get a piece of paper and pen and find a comfortable, quiet place to sit. Take four very deep breaths, taking air in through the nose and exhaling it through the mouth. Close your eyes and call your awareness to your sacred center. Picture it as a room. What does it look like? Feel like? Is it full? Or empty? Is it decorated or plain? Do you feel comfortable there, or uncomfortable? Is there anyone else in the room? If so, who?

Now, take note of any other details about your room, its contents, and how it makes you feel to be there. Don't worry about the images that come; just take detailed notes of them. If no images come, become aware of your thoughts and feelings during this process. If you get nothing but a blank screen, that's okay too; just sit taking deep breaths for the fifteen minutes. Consider doing this awareness session three days in a row. Remember, there is no way you can do this wrong; and the more frequently you do this ritual, the more your awareness will shift.

The Slayer's Altar: I Am Safe

Affirmation: I am safe to accept myself exactly as I am in this moment and be at peace.

What you will need:
- Orange candle
- Your favorite fresh flower
- A picture of yourself
- The affirmation written on a piece of paper

Place everything on the altar and light the candle for at least one hour a day. Keep a daily altar journal and document everything that you think and feel as it relates to the affirmation. Take time daily to notice your thoughts and feelings, as well as what subjects or experiences elicit the greatest emotional responses. When the altar is complete (that is, when the candle has burned down to the socket), bury the wilted flower in your garden or wrap it gently in a paper towel and throw it in a dumpster away from your home.

PART THREE

YOU KNOW YOU WANT IT

Demons are sexy

The Slayer's Weapons:

Self-Control, Non-Judgment, Self-Esteem, Faith, Self-Pity, Self-Awareness

NINA
BRUCE
LAUDANUM
-POISON-

The Story of Nina Broussard

In 1922, she was born Constantina Broussard, in the Bottomlands of Mississippi. A girl of mixed race, she had the best features of each. At least that's what they said, but still she had no friends. While the abomination of discrimination in the United States was fiercely looked down upon by quite an elite crowd, in most places they didn't hesitate to hold up a paper bag next to Nina's face to determine her eligibility of entrance. Bigotry was the way of the day, and racism was the biggest racket going.

Nina was fairly lucky. As she grew up, folks just didn't seem to bother her much. Most days she had no supervision and would hang out on the porch of the local general store, singing her little heart out. Nina knew she was meant for something different than this. She was born of a father who was third-generation emancipated; her Creole mama never quite recovered from her childhood. Both now deceased, Nina stayed with the only relative she had, her ailing grandmother, who was reaching the end of her tenure here on this side. Nina understood that when she was gone, there'd be no one. Singing was the only thing that brought her spirit solace.

As fate would have it, a man named Nicki Tulio happened upon that porch one day. The minute Nina and Nicki laid eyes on each other there was...something—an attraction, a knowing, a kindred spirit, maybe even a love based on need. Nina approached him; he thought she could really sing. After buying her a hot meal and spending a good portion of the day with her, filling her with stories of the good life, she said goodbye to her grandmother, packed a bag, and left with Nicki for New Orleans.

The one and only Nicoli "Nicki" Tulio, who owned a string of nightclubs in New Orleans, New York, Chicago, and Philadelphia, discovered Nina when she was fifteen. He'd heard her before he saw her, but when he laid eyes on Nina his mouth watered. She was his favorite age.

Nicki was a fairly swarthy man with moderately refined features. Elegantly stout, he stood about 5'9". Although Nicki never admitted it to anyone, he was Romani, born Nicoli Lupei. His proud, nomadic people originally came from the Punjab region of India, then migrating all over the world. The Romani had been enslaved for hundreds of years and then deeply persecuted by the Nazi's all over Europe. The Romani were looked upon as pariahs and completely excluded from mainstream society wherever they went. Nicki arrived in America almost two decades before WWII, when he was eighteen. He was lucky to immigrate when he did. The Nazis took out half the Romani population in Eastern Europe, including the Lupei family. Like Nina, Nicki was alone in the world.

He settled in Chicago and learned quickly it was better to be Italian—not a lot better, but better—and changed his name. Nicki was a real salesman and knew he could get in with the right people in the right places. That would be the only way he'd survive. He got his start in the meat-packing industry and became a made-man within a decade. Soon he'd built a reputation for himself that secured safe passage almost anywhere. He had a real penchant for giving people what they liked: illusions of grandeur. Nicki could make anything seem good, even himself.

> Singing was the only thing that brought her spirit solace.

He promised, "Mark my words, Nina, you're going to be a big star, with all the talent you have—a real winner."

No one had ever spoken to her in that way before.

If nothing else, Nicki Tulio was telling the truth. Within six months, he'd taken her virginity; in a year's time, he changed her name to *Nina Bruce*; and within two years, she was a jazz singer headlining at all his clubs. Soon enough he would introduce her to heroin, but that would come later.

Nina liked the good life. She thought the jewels and sequins suited her, and even though she had to do what Nicki liked, she didn't mind. She was queen at all the clubs, getting to use the front door even when she wasn't with Nicki.

Their problems began when she was headlining in New York City. Something about the city changed him, and he was getting rougher and meaner. As hard as she tried to keep up with his sexual proclivities, she just couldn't. Sometimes he would leave her bound and gagged for days—until, of course, the next gig. This time they were going to be in New York for at least six months, and she didn't know how she was going to get through it, let alone hide it.

Nicki had so many things going on that he hadn't noticed the depression she was in. Finally, when he recognized it, he decided to take matters into his own hands by rolling a cigarette for her with a bit of opium. It did change her mood, and she liked it. She never really saw her addiction coming. First, it was opium, then cocaine, then heroin, then anything else—and of course she always enjoyed a well poured Manhattan, although mint juleps were her favorite, a little taste of home.

It was her twenty-third birthday and the beginning of the end. It was 1945 on a cool October night with a slight rain; the dark and glistening city streets seemed so peaceful. By this time she was completely strung out and just about everyone knew. Christopher Coleridge, who'd played piano for her since the beginning and had his love unrequited for the same amount of time, noticed he hadn't seen her for a while. After the second set, she'd flown into a rage when Nicki brought a new mulatto girl with him to the club. He had never done that before.

Nina didn't often use needles, and was usually quite careful when administrating her needs; this time she was too angry to pay attention. Christopher found her in the dressing room with a half-full syringe still in her arm. She was lucky; she passed out before she pushed all of it. Otherwise it would have been the literal death of her.

Christopher and the bass player got her to her feet and around the corner to Christopher's apartment on the second floor. How was it that a woman could take so much abuse, degradation, and disrespect but then lose her mind when she was replaced, he wondered. One would think she'd be relieved.

The bass player knew all about Nicki's way: he'd worked at the club for many years and seen Nicki do this a few times with others. They put her in the shower, slumping her to the floor and turning it on.

"Man, I got a late hit," said the bass player, and with a look and a firm pat on Christopher's shoulder, he was gone.

It took a couple of days to get her right again, with Christopher doting on her as if she were an infant. Christopher was a real looker, but unfortunately, the way he looked in that zoot suit couldn't help him now. He was young and a little naïve so it was almost like the blind leading the blind. It was awhile before she could keep down solid food. He'd snuck over to her place to gather some clothing when he was sure no one would notice. Horrified at the mess he saw, he grabbed a few things and got out of there. He liked to see her in plain cotton dresses thinking they brought out her beauty more than the sequins. The two had never spent this much time together and had seven more days before the next big show started.

Nicki was calling around town trying to find her. He always knew where she was, but this time only the bass player knew, and he wasn't saying anything.

Nina's strong affection for Christopher was growing. He was so helpful. Love wasn't really something Nina understood—she only understood survival. The two of them moved about those next seven days spending them carefully as if they were pure gold, cooking meals and talking. Her drug intake was considerably less, but they had an understanding: it would always be a part of this life.

On the sixth day, Christopher put her in a taxi in the dead of night, and she arrived home to find a dismal disgusting mess. She too was horrified. The stench emanating from the bathroom was undeniable. Almost every dress she owned was strewn on the floor from her manic indecision, and the kitchen was breeding a trail of maggots from something that had fallen behind the counter. Nina fell to the floor and wept, witnessing how she'd been living. The smells got to her the most. Finally, she picked herself up off the floor and cleaned and cleaned until the whole place was spotless. She put the cuffs, muzzle, ropes, leashes, whips, and chains in a box and put them on the curb to be taken away with the rest of the trash. It was a new day. The sun was out.

"And now give a warm round of applause to tonight's main attraction: the undeniable Nina Bruce," announced the MC.

Walking out onto the stage that night she felt different, clearer. Walking into the club had been different too. She was no longer allowed to use the front door.

Nicki ignored her for months. Although he made himself scarce, his presence was always felt; No more carte blanche, no more beatings, no more fancy dinners, no more drugs. Everything else she could handle, but she didn't make enough money to satisfy her habit. For that matter, she didn't always get paid, and no one was willing to cross Nicki who by that time ran everything in the club, the neighborhood, and almost half the city.

Christopher did his best to keep her fixed up without Nicki finding out, but it was difficult because Nicki's reach was wide and far. One thing Christopher did know was all of Nicki Tulio's enemies. Nicki had a reputation as a benevolent gangster, and he didn't discriminate—he wanted everybody's money.

Some say it was his rise and fall. Even sworn enemies of the family were allowed in Nicki's club. It was a safe house of sorts. By and large, it was the reason for the unusual peace throughout the city—that and the war. But after the end of WW II circumstances were rapidly changing. Now that the war economy was over, times were better for some and worse for others. Nina and Christopher spoke of marriage even though it wasn't anything she'd ever considered before. She never thought it would happen for her.

> Walking out onto the stage that night she felt different, clearer. Walking into the club had been different too.

Christopher had been getting heroin from one of Nicki's competitors uptown, who'd been looking to break into the downtown drug territory for a while. His name was Bernie Range, and his family had been the biggest producers of pornography in New York City for three generations since migrating from France. He had a burgeoning drug racket uptown, but he wanted more. He wanted Tulio's.

Bernie was young and smart, charming and elegant, vicious and unrelenting—he always got what he wanted. Bernie Range even frightened his own family. The rumor was he killed two of his uncles to take over the family business and countless small-time drug dealers, usurping the trade uptown. Bernard Range wasn't afraid to do what it took.

Bernie had eyes everywhere and had taken a liking to Tulio's downtown. And like everyone else, he had become quite smitten with the musical stylings of Nina Bruce. Everyone in town knew that she was Nicki's girl, but when he saw her look at Christopher on stage, he wondered how no one seemed to know.

One night he sent his driver, Genus, for Christopher. He brought him to a speakeasy on 127th and Lenox. It was four a.m. and the club was just getting started. Christopher was led back into a private room where Bernie was enjoying some champagne watching the ladies dance.

"I believe you and I have some common goals," said Range. "You don't need to say a thing, just listen."

Christopher was sitting as a glass was poured for him.

"I know about your relationship with Nina Bruce, I know that if you stay here neither of you will ever be free from Nicki Tulio. I am going to help you with two things. Safe passage to Paris—I think they'll just love the two of you there and you'll do well—and I will make sure that Nina gets what she needs."

Christopher's heart began to pound as he gulped down some champagne. There was no hiding it; his nerves were obvious.

"What I need from you is Nicki Tulio's whereabouts at all times and your discretion. Can you do that?"

Without hesitation, Christopher responded, "I can."

"Genus, get this gentleman a nice bottle to take with him and see that he gets home safely."

Genus was standing there with his overcoat and escorted him back to the waiting car, picking up a bottle on the way as he'd been instructed. Christopher's mind was overrun with thoughts all the way home.

As the months went by, Christopher shared every bit of information he could on Nicki's whereabouts. He'd not told a soul about their meeting, not even Nina. Meanwhile, she knew the danger they'd be in if Nicki found out about their relationship, so she was doing her best to play along, occasionally preforming fellatio on Nicki when he popped his head into the club. He stopped by at ten p.m. like clockwork to pick up the first take of the night. Nicki didn't like to have extra cash laying around. It appeared that the other girl was taking the brunt of his aggression, so when he saw Nina, his need to humiliate her was uncommonly low. He even seemed nice on occasion and asked her how she was, leaving her a C-note and a little bottle of laudanum.

One night, however, something was different. It was one of the hottest summer nights on record, and the street outside the club was particularly malodorous with sweat, cologne, and urine. Nina was having a difficult time. It was taking forever for her new life to start, and the old life was getting to her. She hadn't been fixed up in more than two days, so when Nicki showed up for the nightly take, she was particularly pitiful: standing in the alley at the back entrance, bobbing at the knees, smoking a cigarette, sweating, and trembling. She was barely wearing her blue sequined dress, and her wig was askew.

Nicki always wore suits, but tonight he wore a white, crispy, short-sleeved shirt with the sleeves rolled up with black straight-legged pants and his wing tips. He didn't much notice the gut that hung over the top of his pants. He pulled up to the back door for the money pickup. The minute she saw him she practically dove into the back of the Clipper.

"Hi baby, did you miss me, did you miss your Nina?" she said as she went directly for his zipper. "I need some baby, I really need some—"

Out of the shadows from both sides of the alley, came two men with machine guns, shooting the Clipper from both ends. The barrage of fire lasted no more than seconds and in a flash the men had disappeared back into the night. Christopher heard the shots and came running, along with a couple of Nicki's guys.

"No!" he screamed.

The door to the Clipper was open, and there was Nina half-dressed and huddled over Nicki. It was clear she'd taken a few of the bullets meant for him. She was gone, the driver was dead, but Nicki Tulio was still breathing. Christopher grabbed her and yanked her from the car, the force of her moving body shoving him backwards. Hc fcll against the wall, holding tightly to Nina. Christopher couldn't let her be remembered that way. He wept as he held her until the police arrived.

It wasn't supposed to go like this.

Nina and Christopher spoke of marriage, but it wasn't anything she'd ever considered before. She just didn't think it would happen for her.

But it couldn't have gone better for Bernard Range III. Within days he moved in, taking out key people in Nicki's drug business all below Varick St., and within three months he'd bought the club, keeping the name Tulio's for nostalgia. As for Christopher, Bernie held to his agreement and sent him to Paris, setting him up with whatever he needed. He was a real class-act that way. Although Nicki Tulio lived, he never had much of a life after that.

The Slayer's Path: Self-Control

Sometimes people are functioning from a low place and trying to upgrade, but are influenced by entities that won't allow them to do so. It's possible for this person to be delivered from the entity that influences them and witness what appears to be a miraculous change in their behavior. But in fact, it's not miraculous at all. In general, people can and will be delivered from their demons when their desire for personal evolution hits critical mass, when 51 percent of their physical, emotional, mental, and spiritual being desires an expansion into their next level of higher-mindedness. They will do this by seeking to understand love and compassion in every situation, therefore upgrading their tendencies, thoughts, and reactions over time until they do not have on any level, a compulsion to attract, participate in, or perpetuate any lower-minded actions. And this, my friends, is a journey of lifetimes. All you can do is your best.

Men, women, and connection

In intimate situations—whether it is sexual, emotional, mental, or spiritual—there is an energetic cord connecting the two people. Through this cord of energy both parties transfer or trade their spiritual essence. When a person is developing spiritually they will be processing a lot of energy on the emotional and mental levels, and often not have a complete grasp of what they need and energetically take from others. You might have heard about a person in this place being referred to as an energy sucker, vampire, or drain. And frankly, to call them such is unkind and lacks compassion.

However, as we've spoken of before, the more negative or harsh the response, the more needed and powerful the message. When it comes to cording, both parties are complicit. There is always some sort of exchange. When we connect in this way, we do so for a reason, and only the recognition of that will release you from the cord permanently. Being willing to look at what you're receiving or what your contribution is and why you're willing to give and receive it, is the resolution.

Having a common philosophy or need is most likely the connection. If this is the case, and you're corded to someone, you can transfer entities as well. Rest assured that whatever you take on you are perfectly equipped to deliver of your own volition.

> Cord Cutting Visualization: See the cord between you and your partner, and notice where in your body it is connected. Calling in St. Michael (or whomever works best for you) here is optimum but not mandatory. Now, visualize the cord being cut with a large pair of scissors. See the cord fall away from both of you. And finally, visualize white light coming into your body via the crown chakra and filling the space where the cord had been.

Sex, power, and the devil

When people are in need, sex becomes a ritual to gain power. The deep desire to procreate encoded in our DNA requires it at a very basic level. When a person is functioning from a place of survival, he only sees his needs getting met, not the impact of his actions. Demons can embellish this need and influence you until the need is met, and the devil will always justify it for you. Ultimately, however, you will wake up from the dream, break the spell you are under, or be released from the mojo at work. Everyone is responsible for their actions. Nonetheless, the amount of power a demon can have when you are in a position of need or desire is tremendous. The devil cannot actually hurt you in any way: he specializes in getting you to hurt or sabotage yourself.

Sex can easily be used to transfer emotions other than love and affection such as helplessness, anger, grief, or fear. Obviously, this is not true for all sexual acts, but it definitely applies to the sex we are talking about here. There is something that people often do, called *sharing the burden*. Energetically and emotionally, when we engage in sexuality and intimacy, there is a connection of spirit and a transfer of burden, from one partner to another. The burden can be a denser emotion, an entity of some sort, or an energetic cord that connects you to this sexual partner until it is recognized and removed and the relationship is resolved.

Ladies and gentlemen with tails

Over the years when working with clients, a popular topic of discussion is sex and relationships. Every time that I can remember, when I see someone has been afflicted in this way, and I've said "Awe...did he/she have a tail?" I get one of two responses: *Yes, definitely* or a wide-eyed chuckle because people instinctively know when they're having sex with someone who's afflicted with an entity (sometimes the entity even has a tail) or when they are afflicted themselves. The experience is undeniable.

My advice: move away from the tail. Trust me, I've known a few *men with tails*. Sex and relationships with these people will always be about control or survival, until they are required or endowed with the impetus to evolve, forgive, and become their higher self. Adages like *You teach people how to treat you* are accurate in this circumstance. The circumstances look like rape, partner abuse/violence, and antisocial personality disorder on the low end and manipulation, infidelity, bondage and discipline, sadomasochism, or narcissism on the high end.

Only when you can bring compassion and love into your sexuality do you begin to transform your reptilian urges and move beyond a need to procreate for the purposes of perpetuating the species. Requiring yourself to consider the needs of others and understanding your contributions to every situation are keys to bringing love.

Sexual entities without human hosts

Many folks are shocked to know that there are energetic entities that can have sex with you. This kind of attack is more common than you'd think but rarer than other types of attack. People who experience this often have great shame about it because it can illicit feelings of arousal like any other sexual encounter. They may never address it or tell anyone.

The entities that attack in this way aren't necessarily demonic in nature, they can be earthbound spirits, or energetically strong relationships from the past. Know that if this sort of attack is happening to you, it is personal and you are empowered to transform it yourself. A sexual attack is intended to get your attention in some way and an opportunity to overcome and transform your shame.

I've known people who've had relationships with energetic beings and sustained them for long periods of time. Often times this has been a coping strategy put in place to avoid grieving past sexual abuse. Although it can be affective for a while, inevitably, as a person heals they begin to enter back into their physical lives therefore learning to reestablish physical relationships on all levels, including romantic ones. They must eventually change or discontinue the relationship with the entity.

Healing required

The process of healing can appear to happen overnight or over lifetimes, it depends on where you begin your perspective. When you happen upon or attract this sort of thing, it is because something within your spiritual lineage needs to be healed and evolved into a more expanded cycle of needs. Don't judge yourself or others. Just do the work. No matter what form of sexual entity or relationship you have to them, it is your responsibility to set boundaries. It is *your* body.

I had seen these creatures in dreams or sensed their presence through others, but the first time I saw a tail was quite profound. I had entered into a relationship with a crack addict. He was newly sober—so he said—for almost a year. He seemed to be doing the work, and I appreciated many of his qualities, especially his compassion, work ethic, and humor. But, he was a man in his forties who was deeply abused as a child and had been addicted from the age of twelve. I definitely entered into the relationship with open eyes.

I didn't know at the time he'd been to at least twenty recovery and rehabilitation centers and that he'd had several mental health diagnoses. Somehow he had emerged from all of those years of drug use without the obvious neurological tremors that often occur in people that have used drugs for a long period of time. Crack users specifically get a neural tick that looks like they are chewing gum.

When you happen upon or attract this sort of thing, it is because it is something within your spiritual lineage that needs to be healed and evolved into a more expanded cycle of needs. Don't judge yourself or others. Just do the work.

One day he woke up in a bit of a manic frenzy and wanted to take a spin in the sheets. As he mounted me, I immediately lost track of his actions because my focus was drawn to the enormous creature that surrounded him. I was in awe to witness such a thing, almost as if I were mesmerized. It looked like a human-sized dino-lizard with strong, short legs and a long, wide tail. I hadn't noticed the increasing intensity, velocity, and force with which he was thrusting into me until he slammed into my "back door," if you will. The excruciating pain woke me up, and I reeled out from under him into the little four-by-four bathroom a few feet away. Sitting on the toilet, I promptly passed out from the pain. I proceeded to fall over onto the floor, hitting the door and slamming it shut.

When I came to, I got up from the bathroom floor, went into the room where he was sitting watching television, and said, "What the @#$%! Why didn't you help me? I passed out in there."

And his response took my breath away:

"I thought you were mad at me, that's why you slammed the door."

And you didn't hear the thud of my body hitting the floor? I thought.

In a gentle voice I replied, "I didn't slam the door, I passed out from the pain."

His face turned red as he apologized, and we both chuckled as I limped over to the bed and struggled to sit comfortably. I knew then, that I had to walk away from the tail.

Livin' the dream

Living the dream is being in a dense creative space where you are going with the flow of the circumstances you are surrounded by, circumstances created either by you or by someone else. It's what people talk about when they're under a spell. Common circumstances in which this feeling occur are at a concert by a megastar, a mass riot, a political rally, or a circumstance in which a person is focusing their charisma or will-power upon another.

Charisma is your emotional/sexual energy being transmitted through your words and actions. (This energy originates from your second and third chakras through your fourth or fifth chakras.) It's why when we are in a vulnerable state we are susceptible to the leanings of those around us. Some children and adults are particularly vulnerable: those who are abused, addicted, confused, or grief stricken, just to name a few.

Waking up from the dream

I want to be clear here: the people living the dream still have choice, awareness, and usually know the difference between right and wrong. It's that the circumstances appear to closely match their desires or at least begin that way. While living the dream can be positive in nature, beautiful, creative, and miraculous, if living the dream is connected to lower desires or if entities are attached in the process, then experiencing this delusional state can quickly move in an unexpected direction. Sometimes, leaving behind irreconcilable results. Being in this particular spiritual and energetic state can be very dangerous if the dream dynamic includes fear, love, power, hatred, justice, kinship, relief, or revenge to name a few.

Two very important things to remember: First, a person in this state is highly receptive in the telepathic realm. And second, such a person will wake up when their dream is interrupted, which can be caused by anything from a small interruption or telepathic instruction, to an impactful intrusion or trauma. If you find yourself in this situation it is important to always question your thoughts, ideas, or actions to make sure that you have considered fully the consequences in your rational mind.

Of course, those mostly impacted in this way aren't always able to do this. If you are a person who constantly finds yourself in situations that appear not to be of your own making, then you've got to investigate why that is. The affirmation I use to bring up this information is: *I am awake and completely present on all levels in this moment.* Repeating this and having it written in your environment will open up your awareness to the parts of the process or *seduction* that may have previously escaped you.

Even if there is love

Love doesn't mean sacrificing your life because someone is troubled and they deserve love too. Love means setting boundaries, requiring equality, and taking responsibility for healing yourself of your deep karmic patterns. Sometimes love means walking away from people who are unable to take responsibility for themselves and their actions. You don't stop loving them, you just stop allowing harm to yourself in any way. The more you require upgraded thoughts, actions, and behaviors of yourself and others, the more healing begins to take place, transforming the spiritual and then eventually the neurological imprints that predispose you to self-sabotage.

> Love means setting boundaries, requiring equality, and taking responsibility for healing yourself of your deep karmic patterns. Sometimes love means walking away from people who are unable to take responsibility for themselves and their actions.

It was one dark night: Janae's story

Janae arrived back at home one night after having drinks with a few colleagues from work. It seemed like any other night to her husband. But indeed, this was no ordinary night for either of them.

"I'm going to take a quick bath before I come to bed," Janae said to her husband.

After about ten minutes, Jeff heard sobbing coming from the bathroom. He walked to the door, "Are you okay, Janae?"

"Yes, I'm okay...Fuck you, you stupid prick...I'm going to kill your little whore."

"What?" Jeff asked.

He couldn't quite believe what he heard. So, he opened the door, and found Janae lifting a bottle of Drano to her lips.

"What are you doing?" he gasped, as he ran to her, snatching the bottle out of her hands.

Again, she began to sob, saying, "I don't know what's wrong with me. Give me that fucking bottle you asshole." And then she made a growling sound.

Jeff was in shock, he didn't know what was going on, and he had never seen his wife act this way.

I'd met Janae several years before and was now working with her on spiritual development. When we met she'd been on a yearlong bender with methamphetamine and other drugs; she was about a year sober. She'd been doing really well, but was often easily influenced by the people with whom she spent time. When she decided to get sober, she let go of most of the friends she'd accumulated during her drug use. At this point, she'd gotten herself into a support group, had a new job and an amazing husband.

I had one concern: a new fellow joined the firm where Janae was an attorney. He was charismatic, striking, definitely afflicted, and up to no good. That was my initial instinct after meeting him at a visit to Janae's office. Even worse, he lived near Janae and they could carpool to work. In hindsight he was most likely a sociopath and she was his next target. At the time, however, he seemed to be quite taken with her. Since joining the firm, he'd asked Janae to join him for drinks after work twice, telling her he didn't have any friends in the city as he'd just moved from San Francisco.

"Of course it's totally platonic," he said.

The Slayer's Path: **Self-Control**

One night, he, Janae, and a few others from the office went to a little night club around the corner, where he dropped some Ecstasy—a drug that promotes giddy, loving, reckless, and sexy feelings—into her drink. One by one, all the other work friends were gone, and it was just the two of them and Janae was as high as a kite.

She excused herself and went to the ladies' room; she found him in the bathroom waiting for her as she exited the stall. He grabbed her by the hair and kissed her; then pushing her to her knees, he shoved his erection in her mouth, and held her head in place until he was finished. He helped her clean herself up and then drove her home.

It was about two in the morning when I got the call. Janae was under a full demonic attack. Cathy and Margo were fellow colleagues whom I called when I needed help with extreme circumstances. Margo and I decided to meet at Cathy's house. We were the on-call deliverance team. I brought my deliverance kit, which consisted of some courage, a pack of clove cigarettes, some cinnamon creamer for the coffee, and a few choice quartz crystals. Margo had her sense of humor, a Bible, a cross, some holy water, and two packs of cigarettes. Cathy was equipped with her expertise (this wasn't her first rodeo), snacks, an entire carton of cigarettes, and, of course, a full pot of hot coffee. It was going to be a long night.

> Demons will play upon any issues you may have. They are intuitive and instinctive in that way.

Janae's husband had wrapped her, writhing and screaming, in a blanket and during the drive to Cathy's house she had calmed down quite a bit and was mostly just weeping. She had no conscious idea of what was happening to her because it appeared that an aspect of her personality had disassociated from the main alter was deeply afflicted, and a demon had taken possession.

As soon as they arrived, we found some clothes for Janae to wear and got her some coffee. We sent her husband to the other room and soon he was fast asleep. (It's fairly common for a family member to completely retreat until the conflict is over.) We wrapped Janae in warm blankets and began the discussion with her and the entity. Over the course of about four hours, we listened to the vulgar machinations of the demon. He called me every name in the book, told me that I'd never amount to anything, that no one loved me, and (of course) that I was fat.

Demons will play upon any issues you may have. They are intuitive and instinctive in that way. Of course, I wasn't the only lady in the room that got ridiculed, and thankfully these women were hilarious. I remember seeing Cathy with a lit cigarette in her mouth, as the demon blurted out one of the vicious barbs pointed at her.

"Oh yeah?" she said as she topped off my coffee cup with a fresh pot.

I am not going to say that the experience wasn't at times scary, nerve-racking, or adrenaline-filled, but once you get over the fact that these things really exist in this way, you begin to understand that most demons are bullies like any others—sometimes silly, ignorant, and insecure. And I tell you what, we laughed a lot that night. We also prayed and inevitably we were able to summon Janae's inner strength and coax that demon into the light with St. Michael.

Janae and I debriefed a few days later. It would take a long time for her to reckon the many levels of that experience and why it happened to her. She is now living a peaceful life with her husband and three kids.

The Devil Wants to Keep You Confused

When you are caught off guard, it is common to make uninformed choices, which often bring unwanted results and circumstances. But before you can really learn to take control of yourself and your life, you need to understand why you are attracted to and desire the things you do.

When people are looking to protect themselves and remain safe, they may misread a situation. Today, we talk a lot about self-esteem, which energetically is guided by the first layer of your aura; we call it the *body double*. It is the part of your energy that keeps a record of your physical habits. It is generated by the soul's memory: the thought-forms and emotional imprints contained in the soul. It also holds the traditional reactions and behaviors you have for how the people, places, and things in your life react to your soul energy. For example, let's say there is a baby born into the welfare system. This baby is the fourth generation of family to grow-up under this government program with the limited ways and means it provides. We will call this baby, Geri.

Now, let's say Geri's mom is depressed, grieving multiple losses or traumas throughout her life and really only thinks about how she can continue to get her monthly check to stay afloat. Her goals are based upon the rules and regulations set forth by the program and are facilitated by her social worker to whom she is accountable through sometimes weekly, monthly, or quarterly visits. This becomes her cycle of esteem, and her energy body will begin to mimic its restrictions and possibilities.

> IF WE DO NOT FEEL WORTHY OF IT, EVEN GOOD FORTUNE CAN BECOME OUR WORST ENEMY. SIMILARLY, MANY REHAB PROGRAMS FAIL BECAUSE THEY FOCUS ON CHANGING THE ADDICTIVE BEHAVIOR RATHER THAN ON THE DISTRACTION FROM ONE'S INTRINSIC SELF-WORTH THAT THE ADDICTIVE BEHAVIOR PROVIDES.
>
> DR. MARIO MARTINEZ, *THE MINDBODY CODE: HOW TO CHANGE THE BELIEFS THAT LIMIT YOUR HEALTH, LONGEVITY, AND SUCCESS*

Cycle of esteem

Your cycle of esteem is your body double's memory of all that has happened before; your habits are often triggered by the seasons or reoccurring events such as religious holidays or a birthday. Geri's mom has a cycle of esteem based on her accountability to the social worker who approves her monthly welfare check. Her emotions are driven based on this cycle. As the day draws near for her visit, she becomes anxious, angry, and overwhelmed but then covers that up with extra-loud laughs and wide smiles. She sleeps more and accomplishes less around the house, and then the day before the visit she appears to be a crazed lunatic in a twenty-four-hour cleaning frenzy. She always looks haggard for her visit but doesn't know it, with her lipstick a little off. Her esteem, at this point, is not necessarily based on how she feels about herself, but it sets the parameters of how she can possibly feel about herself. Her cycle of esteem and the habits contained therein only allow for so much feel-good energy and are fraught with adrenaline highs and crashes that do not allow for any real peace.

The sign on your head

Baby Geri is born with an energetic sign on his head: it is the energy that others intuitively read from him. An energetic sign is what you pick up on about a person. As an infant, Geri's soul came into this life in order to overcome hardship and find success outside of his family and circumstance. That is the energetic sign or energy that Geri gives off because it is his soul's pure intent.

Geri's mother's sign says, *Go along to get along*. It is the opposite of Geri's. Here is the beginning of Geri's conflict and the creation of his body's energy, or his body double, due to the combination of his pure intent (to overcome his circumstance and his direct surroundings) and the pervading energy of *Go along to get along*. Now, tell me: will Geri have high self-esteem or low self-esteem?

Geri will always carry the energy of knowing that he can have more, that whatever dreams he may have, he can and will fulfill them. It doesn't matter what his family has, because he can always have more. Most likely we would call that expression one of high self-esteem. But remember, Geri is a baby. How does it make Geri's mom feel being confronted with Geri's expression of having more, when she is satisfied and fearful of just getting enough, and what she gets is reliant on someone else?

Let's say she feels judged by Geri energetically and doesn't really think about how or why. She just reacts to Geri's spiritual confidence with fear and tries her best to make him conform. No matter how she does this, whether she beats him, criticizes him, or just plain ignores him she will be in conflict with him. Geri now has, as a part of his body double, the energy that he isn't good enough. This is the rainbow of Geri.

The pot of gold and the meaning of destiny

The pot of gold at the end of the rainbow is this: Geri will inevitably fulfill his soul's pure intent. And the journey he takes will look—certainly in the view of others—rocky. Geri's self-esteem will be based on his soul's initial information, which directs his first beliefs about himself, giving him a baseline to how his world mirrors his beliefs about himself.

The choices he makes because of this internal conflict become his habits, and they may trigger how people respond to him. It is this exact process of internal struggle that creates situations and feelings that over time will provide the opportunity for the soul's true intent to emerge. This is called destiny.

Now again, is his esteem high or low?

His esteem will be a mixed bag, being a reflection of his inner conflict. We know that he will at his core feel good about himself, but he will also struggle with his ability to manifest that goodness in his world until he frees himself from his environment. Geri, over his lifetime, will make choices out of goodness, confusion, worthiness, and lack. He will be happy and unhappy with himself, and eventually he will accept himself and give himself the freedom to carry out his pure intent. His esteem then is not based on how he feels at any given time about himself, but on his inner desire to seek out who he is and to connect with and fulfill his soul's pure intent however he can. He will learn whatever he needs to in order to accept himself and realize his destiny.

For everyone, it is the same process. It doesn't matter if like Geri, you come from poverty or if you come from means, the process of evolution is the same.

So when we say that someone has low self-esteem, what we mean is that their possibilities and parameters at that time are limited, and this goes with the acknowledgement that those parameters are necessary. They may very well feel great about themselves within those parameters, but as you know with expansion comes change, conflict, and struggle. For everyone, it is the same process. It doesn't matter if like Geri, you come from poverty or if you come from means, the process of evolution is the same. All of us live our lives seeking out our pure intent and realizing our destiny. All of us. Always.

Self-loathing: very costly, use sparingly

Spiritually speaking, self-loathing is a very unique experience of self-acknowledgement at its core. As counterintuitive as it may seem, humans use negativity to get attention. The more dramatic or negative the thought or situation, the more we pay attention. It activates our fight-or-flight adrenaline so that we become hyper-vigilant. People seek to diminish their negative thinking, but the reality is, at the beginning it is the only way we stay present. So, if you find yourself being extremely negative, you may not be paying attention to all the details.

Self-loathing and self-pity

Human beings take in billions of pieces of information all the time. The goal is to access, metabolize, and interpret as much as we need based on our evolution. Imagine for a moment that you are your soul floating around the Universe free and unencumbered by a physical body, and your vision, awareness, and feelings as they are today are all intact. The only thing is missing is the physical responses to those feelings. Now imagine being injected into a little infant body, a little fatty blob of flesh generated for you by your parents, with no soul memory of who you are, just a DNA replica of mostly your mom. Feel the brief moment of devastation that the spirit feels against the body and its inability to express its vast information and experience—that is self-loathing.

There is good news. Self-pity and self-loathing are in the same category, and when you feel them they are powerful tools of regeneration. No subtlety here. When you focus on what you hate or loathe about yourself, you have an arrow pointing to your salvation—if you will only be courageous enough to look.

I work with many people who suffer from addiction, and one such man met his wife at a recovery meeting several years ago. They stayed sober, got married, and had three beautiful children. In those years they went through so much together and stayed sober, but because of all the trials and tribulations, they never really took the time to deal with the parts of themselves that they sought to anesthetize. Slowly but surely, in bits and pieces those parts of themselves came to the forefront once again, as they always do. Eventually, once again he went to rehab, and she was left to take care of their three children on her own. Self-pity, in a fierce way, was not a surprising response to her dilemma. Every day her focus was on how much she was going to miss him, how hard it was for her without him, and how much there was to do now that she had to do it all by herself.

As I listened to her, the self-pity meter was registering off the scale. For a brief minute I was beginning to loathe her, and then I stopped. What was the message here? I had worked with this client for a short time, and all of a sudden the realization came crashing down. Her triggers were abandonment and not having her needs acknowledged. As a child, her needs were never acknowledged and she felt abandoned by all the adults in her life. Eventually, this is what she did to her self through her abuse of drugs.

This circumstance was an echo of exactly where they were when they met with a slight upgrade: a stable home, a good job, three beautiful children, and lots of support systems around them. Now every time she feels sorry for herself, it brings her attention to all these conditions she'd not experienced before. Good things. The devil in this case is the illusion that the state of her affairs remained unchanged. The reality is that things are ever-changing, but we continue to view them through a lens of fear, never transitioning how we see them.

The Slayer's Motto: I Am Perfect Exactly As I Am

Claiming your unified self in its highest form in the present moment creates the opportunities, support, and innovation you need to move forward in your life in the highest and best direction. The terms *highest* and *best,* in this circumstance, are used to train your thinking and to bridge the gap between your lowest common denominator and highest ideal. Repeating this mantra can often be uncomfortable at the beginning as it brings to the surface any vanity or insecurity you may have. The point at which the idea has integrated is when your feelings about it become neutral.

Desire is the beast

Working with those in the cycle of addiction, I am always reminded of what addiction is from a spiritual viewpoint: your *relationship to* desire. The *desire itself* is the beast. It is how you manage your desire that makes the difference. Your relationship to a substance, an object of your desire, or a behavior is seen through the lens of your relationship to desire itself and your ability to be balanced in that relationship. The Buddhists focus on the idea of learning to diminish your cravings and the Catholics focus on the emotion of guilt to bring awareness to what you desire. Both religions are good at pounding this concept into your brain in their own unique way.

> An addict is always wanting more but not ever getting enough, because there isn't ever enough when you always want more.

Our society encourages desire at every stop. Everywhere you look supports immediate gratification and your urge to always want, get, and have more than you do right now. That is how an addict feels all the time. An addict is always wanting more but not ever getting enough, because there isn't ever enough when you always want more. What in the hell do you do with that? Demons infiltrate the confusion, craving, and aggression that desire sometimes brings about.

The wanting

The conversation began with us talking about heroin. My friend said, "You never really get over that wanting."

It made me think. That is addiction: the relationship you have to wanting and desire. Do you get over that wanting? It's like a first love that opens your heart in a way you've not experienced before; it makes you feel incredibly powerful. When you're in it, it is the most magnificent vibration. You fear losing it because you can't imagine having it this good again.

Eventually you assimilate and balance out your response to having the object of your desire. You may not recognize the change and not realize it is your heart that is changing. You think it is all about the object of your desire, and if you just have more, you'll feel the same way you did in the beginning. The adrenaline rush will be the same as your first experience. So, you keep grasping, trying to get back that feeling of openness regarding the object of your desire, but to no avail. You think if you keep doing whatever it was you were doing then eventually you will feel the exact same way. But you don't—ever. That is addiction, your relationship to desire.

Consider that your partnership with desire is very much connected to hormones and other chemicals in your body in addition to behavior, thoughts, and emotions. Dealing with addiction requires you bring all of these levels into balance. The longer you remain in a pattern of addictive behavior the longer it may take to resolve the addictive pattern physiologically, ideologically, emotionally, and spiritually.

The Slayer's Motto: **I Am Perfect Exactly As I Am**

Returning to innocence

Let's dial it back a minute and talk about what's really happening. The Universe creates through a series of expansions and contractions, as we ourselves do. While I suppose the Universe is limited in comparison to the Creator, I am certain there are universes in abundance beyond our comprehension. It is what we believe that is the gateway to our understanding, but once we have a particular set of knowledge we will eventually need to adjust our beliefs to gain more wisdom. This process of transformation is definable and inherent in all life. What's important to know is that It's not only this way for you, but for all living beings. It gives some focus to the we are *One* sentiment.

When I was a young child, I would dream about a tall man with an olive complexion and dark hair who chased me—sometimes in my house, other times in my neighborhood, or different locations I'd not been. What was consistent were his clothes. He always wore black, straight-legged trousers and a white short-sleeved, thin cotton dress shirt with a pocket on the left side with the sleeves rolled up to show his muscular arms. His slicked, black hair was a throwback to another era along with his black leather shoes. He chased me with a filled syringe of what I knew to be heroin. There was no reason for me know about heroin at the age of seven. My parents at the time were drinkers and smokers as it was fashionable, but that habit eventually gave way to the latest diet fad.

At that young age I had an incredible attraction to Janis Joplin: an amazing artist who was as known for her drug use as she was her music. My dad was a disc jockey and had brought home a copy of *Pearl*, Janis Joplin's final album. I would sit and muse at her photos for hours, but I couldn't bring myself to listen to her music because I couldn't bear the pain that flowed through it. The first time I put the record on to listen, I burst into tears after only a minute and had to turn the record player off.

Consequently the man in my dream never caught me. I'd wake up at-times in tears or a cold sweat (from escaping his grasp) but I'd always wake up. Repeatedly, I had this dream all the way through high school. I attribute my repulsion to drug use to it. Most of my friends from early on used pot and other substances, but I always knew that was a door I was trying to close rather than open.

> IT TAKES A LOT OF COURAGE TO RELEASE THE FAMILIAR AND SEEMINGLY SECURE, TO EMBRACE THE NEW. BUT THERE IS NO REAL SECURITY IN WHAT IS NO LONGER MEANINGFUL. THERE IS MORE SECURITY IN THE ADVENTUROUS AND EXCITING, FOR IN MOVEMENT THERE IS LIFE, AND IN CHANGE THERE IS POWER.
>
> ALAN COHEN

The Spiritual Process of Conflict

Conflict is the phase of spiritual process where we start to engage the possibility of change. In preparation for conflict we adopt new philosophies that will support the transition and begin to release old belief systems, people, circumstances, or elements that no longer support the transformation.

Fight the good fight. That phrase has always confused me because is there really a *good* fight? What personifies a good fight for me is inner conflict, the third element in the spiritual process of change. Conflict, and therefore struggle, is the game changer. It is the point in the process where we eventually recognize there really is no struggle, only choice, and the fight is the process of obtaining the tools to make the choice.

Imagine a seed planted under a foot of earth. Now, imagine that seed has feelings and empathize with it. This is a *good fight.* The seed can only focus on his resources at hand, the water and nourishment in the ground and the warmth of the Sun. The seed pushes through and changes every day based on what he sees (the water) and what he doesn't see (the Sun) until he reaches the surface. Breaking ground, the seed must address and adapt to all the other factors now present in his world or parish.

> KUNDALINI—(Sanskrit) is a concentrated field of intelligent, cosmic invisible energy vital to life. It is stored and begins its movement at the base of the spine as a young man or woman begin to evolve. Kundalini has been described as liquid fire or liquid light. The ultimate outcome of kundalini movement in the body is the union of Will, Knowledge, and Action.

Enter the dragon

Our kundalini energy moves through the physical body, energetically opening glands in our endocrine system during different phases of spiritual development. It is our connection to Source in the physical body. When we are experiencing spiritual conflict, we will see physical problems stemming from the endocrine system. Many people who experience chronic depression will also experience chronic fatigue syndrome or evidence of similar imbalances. The easy flow of the life-force energy in the body also regulates the chemicals that help shape how you think and feel. The life-force energy also contributes to mental and emotional stability. Emotional obstacles, extreme emotionalism, lack of mental focus, or inability to sleep can be a result of a kundalini awakening or blocks in the energy body (the chakra system).

Battle of the will

During the phase of conflict, the real battle is with your own willpower, and the struggle is eventually talking yourself out of whatever is no longer working or in your best interest. When you are in conflict, you are completely aware of what the issues are and often at least moderately aware of the resolution. The struggle is to accomplish mastery of the will regarding the situation. We will experience a battle of the will on all levels: spiritually, mentally, emotionally, energetically, and physically. For example, someone who is haunted often knows they are haunted. The struggle for acceptance involves admitting that otherworldly beings exist and facing any fears they may have about it.

Spiritual conflict

Spiritual conflict can be evidenced by intense dreaming, lack of sleep, and experiencing spiritual and paranormal events. Anything from seeing ghosts, experiencing demonic attack, to suffering actual entity influence. When there is a lot of spiritual conflict there is usually a past-life or ancestral component.

Remember that whatever is going on in your spirit will attract more of it to you. Ritual is a helpful practice if you have a lot of spiritual imbalance. The golden rule here is that any spiritual conflict acknowledged and brought into the physical plane can be resolved and released. Entities of any sort must have our permission on some level to participate in our life. Naming it is the first step to releasing it.

Mental conflict

Evidence of conflict on the mental level shows up as extreme opinions, flip-flopping in your opinions, being easily influenced by the belief systems of others, or selective hearing. (The minute you hear a key word that ignites your inner-conflict, you stop listening and assume its meaning.)

Dealing with mental conflict is easiest when managed with structure. Take the idea in conflict and write it down. Now, write possible replacements for the idea and commit three days to *try them on for size.* (Live with them as if they were your truth.) Document your experience and what you thought and felt while weighing each belief as if it were yours for the time. For example, racism, politics, and religion are the top three hot-button topics. Write down each topic with the beliefs you have associated with them. Then, write down next to each belief: Does this belief include or exclude others? Yes or no? Now, write down what purpose such a way of thinking may have, or the possible wisdom obtained by having it.

Emotional conflict

Emotions are the carriers of spirit into the physical world and a way the brain transforms and removes neurons that carry old beliefs. This makes emotion very important to any transition. *Grief* is what we call this phenomenon. In Sanskrit it is called *kriya*, which means a purified action. Our emotions are one of the body's amazing ways of detecting and interpreting usable information.

While working through emotional conflict, it is not uncommon to experience extreme or continual emotion as a part of this process. Crying excessively is to be expected, and embracing it helps you to recover more easily from the kriya. Also, fits of rage or anger are evidence of forward movement. The strategy here is to take notice of what happens five minutes before the anger is triggered. After the fact, focus on what happened and how you would like it to change. The more you add analysis and understanding to this process the less you or your body will have the need for the extreme emotional trigger you experience.

Energetic conflict

Energetic conflict refers directly to behavior and the automatic impulses we have trained ourselves in throughout our lives (our habits). These habits are based on the energetic memory of the first layer of the aura (the body double or etheric layer). The point at which we are ready to make significant changes in our lives and behavior is the time when our energy body resists the most.

Let's say you are a smoker. When you decide to quit smoking, the energy body will still continue sending the impulses of the old behavior, so if you normally had a cigarette after lunch, the craving and impulse will be stronger after lunch. That's why it is best to exchange one habit for a better one.

> Our emotions are one of the body's amazing ways of detecting and interpreting usable information.

Physical conflict

Physical conflict is anything from aches and pains to disease. The physical body is a mirror of all other levels of your energy. Spiritual, mental, or emotional conflict will show up as congenital defects, and chronic or extreme disease. Conflicts that are temporal will show up as illness, aches, or pains much like the child who did not finish his homework will get a sudden stomachache. The good news here is that every physical ailment has a component and connection on another level of energy. If you have a physical imbalance, focus on accessing its origin in spirit, and you can clear the physical imbalance completely. If you have a life-threatening, chronic, or congenital issue, then finding its spiritual origin and restoring peace with it will help you integrate the wisdom of your condition and help you find acceptance in things as they are.

The Slayer's Pact: Require Love to Prevail

Finding peace and accepting yourself as you are in any moment is the key to conflict resolution. When you see your struggle as your best friend you can begin to work with your own higher intelligence, releasing old, unneeded information and integrating new wisdom brought to you by the struggle. During any time of conflict, it is incredibly important to learn to take care of your physical body with nutrition, body work (massage, acupuncture, acupressure, e.g.), and energy medicine. Also, working with an altar and affirmations is helpful to align with the new desired energy.

> Believe in your dreams and you will lose yourself. Believe in yourself and you become your dreams.
>
> Nina Bruce

How I met Nina Bruce

The impact of this past-life on my present one has been profound. From earliest childhood I was haunted with the life of Nina Bruce and her addiction. Those soul memories affected the way I perceived relationships, drugs, men, music, and myself on so many levels. For example, I didn't believe I would live to see my twenty-fifth year. Nina lived until she was twenty-five years old and died of a fatal gunshot wound. It was her memory constantly gnawing at my sub-conscious, telling me life was short and to live it fully.

It also provoked special responses from the world outside of me. In certain situations people seemed to know me, yet we'd never met. They would include me in unlikely groups or by the same token exclude me, sometimes working in my favor and sometimes not. Either way, there was always a familiarity in the subtle dynamics of my relationships with others that could not be explained in any other way but by means of our spiritual common denominator.

Also, I have vivid memories of some of the deep, inner conflicts I would have, especially regarding music and singing. I loved music and loved to sing and perform but was in deep spiritual conflict with it. Around the age of eleven, I was with my childhood friend Kelly singing Melissa Manchester as loudly as we could into a hairbrush. I thought to myself, *I don't ever want to be a singer—yuck*. The pain I heard in the voices of many singers was often unbearable for me to process. Even at that age, I had awareness of what a strange thought it was to think about *not* being something, and it stuck with me.

My earliest memory connected to the life of Nina Bruce was the recurring dream I mentioned before. Every time I'd have that dream he'd be chasing me in a new place: my elementary school, my room, the grocery store, and even hiding behind the big maple tree in the yard down the street. The tree trunk was large enough to hide a person from view. It was pretty frightening for a four-year-old. I don't think I spoke of these dreams to anyone until I was at least thirty. Needless to say, I never felt safe anywhere—at least Nina didn't—and it led to incredible anxiety most of the time.

My relationship with alcohol began from watching my parents and their friends have a couple of martinis, then taking their drinks, getting in the car, and driving off to dinner or a game—it always seemed so glamorous and harmless. My first experience drinking was at the age of ten. Me and a friend got an old tea bag can and filled it with rum and Coke from my folk's liquor cabinet. We walked to the elementary school we attended a few blocks away from my house, at six a.m. on a Sunday morning, and got blottoed. We laughed all the way to Dunkin' Donuts where we ordered sweet-treats and soda. We were sure they would suspect our drunkenness. Of course, it makes perfect sense—two drunk ten-year-olds out at seven a.m. on a Sunday morning.

Even though I drank consistently from that point on, stealing liquor and cigarettes from the home stash, I always knew I had to keep it in moderation. As a twelve-year old, I was ware I had the potential to be an alcoholic and wasn't interested in that road. Surprisingly, I never had the desire to do any other type of drug, and didn't. I said to myself, *You've got too many people in your head already, drugs are a bad idea,* and I always stuck to that sentiment.

I had an innate understanding of the multiple spiritual dimensions that mind-altering substances open you to, and I just didn't participate. In my teen years we were allowed a glass of wine or champagne on holidays, and by the time I was sixteen I would go to happy hour with my mother and her soon-to-be husband. The fake ID I had got me entrance to the local bars where—even though I drank frequently—I was always the controller of the group, staying sober enough to take care of the others and their inebriation. Exposure to drinking in my case, whether through family or friends, was never the impetus towards drinking for me, but it did allow me early on to recognize my power over drinking and drugs, not their power over me.

By the time I moved to New York City at the age of eighteen, I had less interest in drinking; there was a lot more to focus on. Music was both light and dark to me, and NYC was the place I pursued my relationship with jazz and blues. I loved singing to myself, as it was the only thing that brought me peace. All the while, feeling intensely resentful of the music industry and my inability to sing songs without expressing deep pain and grief. I was limited to the music that could carry the weight of my style and voice.

At this point I already had my ghetto tenement flat on 111th and Frederick Douglass Blvd. and just up the street on 118th was a little jazz bar named Betty's where I had my first real dose of Nina Bruce's life. This dimly-lit bar—one street away from a crack house—was the brightest thing on the block in what was a predominantly burned-out neighborhood. I met a musician there one night. He was a short, spindly man, wearing a 1970s brown tweed suit. His name was Cappy.

He was a washed-up trumpet player who was in his late fifties or early sixties but seemed so old and fragile. I knew he drank a lot but was unaware of his cocaine use at the time.

I witnessed a dichotomy in the way people treated him, over the short time we were connected. Everyone he knew seemed to feign respect for him, while at the same time not taking him seriously. Cappy had a memorable career in the music industry and boasted of being a member of the legendary Copasetics. He played with notable musicians like Miles Davis and Art Blakey, and wrote and recorded a lot of music over the decades. In addition, he was a deeply manipulative predator who liked the young, vulnerable ladies—it's my belief your life will inevitably reveal what is concealed in your spirit.

At the time, I was interested in music, attracted to jazz and blues, and enamored by Cappy's charm and swagger even in such a state of dilapidation. Cappy ended every set with, "And you know that...."

> Nina lived until she was twenty-five years old and died of a fatal gunshot wound. It was her memory constantly gnawing at my sub-conscious, telling me life was short and to live it fully.

So when he asked me to get up and sing a song during his set, of course I obliged. This was my first sit-in at a New York City club, and by *club* I mean small, dark, hole-in-the-wall that was the neighborhood haunt. The place where you knew all the regulars. It was the first of a singing experience i would have many times over.

I got up on stage. I was going to sing "Lover Man," the Billie Holiday classic. I gave the band my key, I took the mike and began to sing...and don't remember a thing until I was saying thank you and walking back to my seat. It appears I finished the song, as the few people that night seemed genuine in their applause, but whether the clapping was for my moxie or my performance, I wasn't sure. I did have the tendency to get a little pitchy when I was nervous, but either way I didn't remember singing a note.

After that night Cappy wanted to make me his protégé and from that point on introduced me as such to people at the clubs.

"May I present my protégé, Ms. Tracee Dunblazier," he'd say.

It was hilariously devastating to see the looks on people's faces, especially the ones who knew his game with young women. I suspected he'd had many "protégés."

At the time, I didn't fully comprehend why, when he called me that, it inspired anger and disdain. The picture it painted in my mind—of a woman in a navy-blue, sequined dress standing in the spotlight—was sickening to me.

I will never be that, I thought to myself.

Cappy offered to teach me music theory, but spending any sort of time with him became burdensome as it was impossible for him not to talk about his penis, sex, or my vagina, at some point. It was amazing how he could work them into a conversation about music. The first time, I laughed; the second time, I told him to stop; the third time—when he told me about the police being called to his house by one of his young students with whom he'd had sex—I was done.

"And you know that...."

The Slayer's Path: **Require Love to Prevail**

Love Is the Great Equalizer

The New York years were very empowering for me, while even the thought and anticipation of moving to Los Angeles brought great trepidation. I think it was the feeling of impending deep soul healing, the emerging past-life memories into my consciousness.

There are two ways to receive a past-life memory. The first way is to receive a vision, memory, or dream. The second way is to relive or re-experience the memory as if it is happening now. Even though you have the awareness that it's not your current situation, you feel every bit of it as if it were, usually just through your emotions, but the pain can be physical as well. The most enduring of these memories for me was going through the heroin detox I was not able to undergo within Nina

Bruce's life and, as I said, the disbelief of living past my mid-twenties in this lifetime.

At the end of her life, Nina Bruce was strung out and beginning to detox from heroin use when she was shot dead at the age of 25. I picked up from there. In this past life recall I wept uncontrollably almost nonstop for almost three weeks, and laid in bed shaking with the worst body aches and sweats I'd ever experienced. At the time I'd been seeing a man whose relationship dynamic with me was very hurtful but I found myself undermined by his charm every time we'd come together. Duke and I had made plans for the afternoon and he'd dropped by to pick me up. Within minutes of his arrival he received a call from someone and said he had to go. Acting as if we'd had no plans at all. My response was surprising to both of us. My rage and grief toppled over and I went hard and fast into a panic attack. Somehow in the process I cut my leg. He noticed that I had a huge gash above my knee and the blood was running down the length of my leg to my ankle.

He began to clean and bandage it. I had no awareness of hitting it. It jolted me into the next level of awareness: I wasn't sick. I was processing the energy of heroin addiction, triggered by Duke's continual disrespect and selfishness, and soon I would be just fine. It took maybe another week from then to feel balanced. For every memory there is a trigger.

After that, having not seen or heard from Duke in several weeks, one night I was out at a fancy dinner with colleagues when he walked into the restaurant with a beautiful model as his date. I lost my breath for a moment. He had the audacity to approach the table to say hello.

I became sick to my stomach and began to perspire; my fate was sealed and the healing imminent. Obviously our relationship in this life wasn't anything like he presented it to be, and my physical and emotional reaction wasn't necessarily rational to the situation either. In truth he was a manipulative, charming liar who warranted the brush off, but instead for several weeks my world fell apart. I reconnected and processed the pain of Nina's life of perpetual disrespect and abuse from Nicki. Those experiences were the beginning of releasing the spiritual and emotional imprints I was unable to process in the previous life.

Then, not too much longer after that I had a dream. It was of a man carrying Nina (I knew the woman in the dream was me) almost unconscious up the stairs to his apartment and putting her in the shower in a white, flowered muslin dress with a forties hairdo.

The man was Christopher Coleridge.

While there were many more releasements to come from other lives, the burden I'd been praying to be delivered from had been lifted. That following week I experienced a lightness unlike anything I could conceive of, and I had peace for the first time.

The Slayer's Altar: Self-Acceptance

Things you'll need:

- Three candles: green, white, and black
- The affirmation written on a piece of paper
- Object representing what you are acknowledging acceptance of
- Glass of water
- Bowl of loose tobacco

Affirmation: "I accept myself completely and fully on all levels. My world is exactly as it should be and I am grateful."

Clean and clear a space for the altar in your bedroom. Light the black candle to embrace your higher self-vision; light the green candle to heal your heart; and light the white candle to purify your mind, body, and spirit of what you no longer need. Place the object on or in front of the altar. Place the water on the left side of the altar and the tobacco on the right. Now place the written affirmation under a candle, sit in front of your altar, and read the affirmation aloud, three times. Keep the altar until the candles burn out. You'll want to have an altar journal to write a bit every day to document what you experience in yourself or notice in your world.

PART FOUR

NO REGRETS

Just Because It's Not Real Doesn't Mean It Didn't Happen

The Slayer's Weapons:

Love, Equality, Control, Truth, and Independence

PULLMAN
PORTER

The Story of Jasmine Lilywhite

Everyone wanted a little bit of Jasmine Lilywhite and understandably so. She was a beautiful silent film star, although maybe a star in movies only your daddy would have watched. Her looks were mesmerizing to all who saw her: men, women, and children. She had the palest skin you'd ever seen, practically see-through; sometimes you could see the blue blood running through her veins. Silky, shiny platinum hair—mostly styled in a short, wavy conk hairdo—framed her face beautifully. Her gentle, heart-shaped, glossy lips and makeup were always done just so. Jasmine stood about five feet six. It really was the perfect size to exclude no one, and people responded to her as if she were royalty. Even the prudes and the Catholics couldn't deny her magnetism as she had a bit of a Mother Mary essence. No one ever really knew where she was born or when she died; all they were left with was the best of her that lived on inside of them.

Jasmine Lilywhite first appeared on the scene in about 1895 in the bohemian Montmartre district of Paris, the seat of burlesque. Although Le Chat Noir was to close within the next couple of years, it was just the start that the twenty-two-year-old Jasmine needed. Everyone who met her thought she was French, and that was the way she liked it. She didn't speak much, but she listened deeply and intently with her heart. She seemed to have a sense of who people were and what they needed. She showed them a bit of themselves by revealing a lot of her, always the most vulnerable part. People thought Jasmine would do anything, and to some maybe that's the way it seemed, but Jasmine always did what she wanted. Le Chat Noir closed in 1897, but from the first time Jasmine took its stage weaving her magic, she had a special fan. The truth was they'd met before.

From the time she left her hometown in Iowa at sixteen, she called herself Jasmine. The locomotive was her father and the Pullman porter her mother; she was deeply loved. The garish clanking of the trains engine became a comforting and enduring sound for her.

The porter, Rodney Strong, hailed from Mississippi and was a third-generation Pullman; he was young and handsome and from the first moment he laid eyes on Jasmine all he wanted was to take care of her—in the proper way of course. You could tell her feelings were mutual.

Somewhere in between Georgia and Mississippi, a man called Golden Eye Johnnie got on the train. Oh, he was charming and to the untrained eye dressed like a businessman. If you looked closely, he was a little dirty around the edges. He stood about five feet four, his skin was a golden light-brown speckled with freckles, and his red, tightly curled hair fit nicely under his cap, only revealing itself in his evenly trimmed beard. For the most part Johnnie seemed to be respected by others, and whatever it was he did for a living he seemed to be successful.

However, there were many crosscurrents with Johnny. Although he was dressed for business, his hands were always strong and rough; while he was really quite charming and funny, he had a controlling cruel streak underneath; and finally he was the most seemingly generous, yet the most truly selfish, man. You never knew who you would get when you ran into Johnnie. And from the time Johnnie got on the train, he'd set his sights on Jasmine.

Jasmine, even at her young age, didn't seem to be too naïve. She was fun and pure of heart but knew what men liked and, most of all, what they needed. Jasmine saw a longing in Johnnie. It was understood that he covered it up with his meanness and his generosity. She knew she could have whatever she wanted from him, because he was so unaware of himself. Johnnie was almost ten years older than she was and always seemed to know what he was doing and where he was going. Even though he only *seemed* to know, she loved his confidence.

From the time they met, Johnnie made lewd comments that should have offended Jasmine. Well, that's what she thought anyway, but they made her loins tingle. He knew he would get her sooner or later.

> She was fun and pure of heart; and the fact was, she knew what men liked and, most of all, what they needed.

The cross-country trip on this train took a couple of weeks because of all the stops they made to load and unload cargo. This gave Jasmine and Johnnie quite a bit of time to get to know each other, and Johnnie did want to know her, so badly in fact it was all he could think about.

One day the train stopped in a fairly remote area. The mockingbirds were mocking loudly that morning, maybe because it seemed so still. The train had to wait for a shipment to arrive so they had several hours to do as they pleased outside.

Johnnie was particularly charming that morning and made an effort to scrub himself clean, something he didn't do often. He arrived at Jasmine's door as the sun was rising, with a nice, hot, dark cup of coffee that he knew she would love. Smelling the coffee through the door, she opened it and reached for the cup with a subtle smile.

Johnnie pulled the cup away. "You can have this if you will go on a picnic with me this morning…in fifteen minutes."

"Okay," she replied, took the cup, and closed the door.

Johnny was speechless and a little breathless. Could it have been that easy? Now he was questioning what could she want from him that she would say yes so easily?

The first sip of thick, black coffee was heaven for her. She could feel his spirit through the door and laughed at how confused he was right now. It was clear she could move him from one place to another with very little effort. She was sure that this very thing would hold some importance for her, although she didn't quite know why. She finished her coffee and dressed and was out the door in thirty minutes. She arrived in the dining car where Johnnie had them prepare a basket for their adventure, and they were off.

The morning was still crisp, and the sun was fully up. On one side of the train was a deeply wooded area and on the other a swamp. Johnnie had been successful with the ladies quite a few times at this stop. That's why he chose it. He did seem confident about the path to a remote, little clearing amongst the trees, about a thirty-minute walk in.

"Have you ever been here?" Jasmine asked.

"No, no I haven't. A gentlemen I met last night was telling me what an invigorating walk it is, and I thought it was something we could both use after being cooped up on this train for so long."

"What a wonderful idea it is!" she exclaimed. She knew he was lying and was okay with it.

They arrived at the appointed spot, and within seconds Johnnie had the blanket spread out on the forest floor. The air was so fresh and still it didn't seem there was anyone around for miles. It was just the two of them, alone at last. Johnnie couldn't contain himself. He already had an erection at the thought of getting her. She smiled ever so gently and batted one eye and then the other, and went straight for the basket. He pulled himself together so as not to seem too gauche.

Offering her a piece of buttered bread, she said, "No, that's yours to eat. I'll have this blueberry muffin."

He didn't know what else to do but take a bite.

They drank some coffee and juice. Soon Johnnie was telling one of the most engaging stories of his travels. They began to laugh so hard they both fell onto the blanket. He leaned over and began to give her an awkward kiss, to which she responded by wiping some butter from the corner of his mouth and then letting him continue. It wasn't very long until his hand was making its way up her thigh. Somehow she knew this wasn't the proper order, but she didn't care. She flinched when he slid his hand down underneath her petticoat to her panties: his hands were so rough that she winced again and squirmed away from him.

Now she was on her stomach, and he thought he'd try kissing the small of her back, just long enough to get her out of that petticoat. This was all feeling nice to her—well, really good, actually—but she'd never tell him. The panties were completely off, and she felt comfortable lying on her stomach until he rubbed those rough hands all the way down her bottom and in between her legs.

"Ouch!" She yelped. "Your hands are too rough!" She knew she hurt his feelings a little as she slid to her knees with her backside still facing him and said, "But you can lick it if you like. I think that would feel best."

Johnnie found himself completely shocked for the first time ever. This didn't seem to be going well, but he wasn't quite sure why.

"Just lick it. Johnnie. I know you'll like it; it tastes like butter."

Now he was a little embarrassed because he'd never done that before, and she was bent over and not looking at him at all. After recognizing his confusion, she reached back with her hands and spread her cheeks and said, "Now, there it is—lick it!"

He did, first with uncertainty and then with furious, wild abandon. It seemed to bring out the generosity in him. Finally, he got her to lie on her back where he could finish what she asked of him more comfortably. And in that moment she knew that although he'd always try, he could never have her.

Johnnie knew that even though it didn't happen right then, it was only a matter of time before he had her.

> He knew that Jasmine was the kind of girl who loved everybody but he knew he had her heart. He felt it every one of those days in her presence.

The sun was now high in the sky, and they needed to get back before supper time. They arrived at the train just as the sun was setting. Rodney Strong was waiting at the door, delighted to see them. Well, delighted to see Jasmine. He was relieved to see the look in her eye as she smiled and said, "Good evening."

She entered the door to the train, and he knew she was still intact. Although he did have an understanding of what kind of girl she was, and that it was really none of his business, he was still relieved. Jasmine promptly got cleaned up and dined by herself so that she could enjoy a little of Mr. Strong's company, even if it was just dinner service.

The remainder of the cross-country journey had its ups and downs. Mostly downs for Johnnie as no matter what he did, he just couldn't get to her. Oh, she let him look at it or touch it on occasion, but this was the beginning of a six-year affair that would never be consummated.

It remained all ups for Rodney. He knew that Jasmine was the kind of girl who loved everybody, truly she did, but he knew he had her heart. He felt it every one of those days in her presence, and the deal was sealed on the last night of her journey when she woke him in the middle of the night, with tears streaming down her face. She had to ask him where she could send him a letter now and again. She didn't quite understand why she was crying, but she knew that missing him would be unbearable. Rodney knew.

As it turned out, Johnnie had a few connections in the silent film business. When they arrived in Los Angeles, he did the best he could to set her up in an apartment near Hollywood Boulevard and give her the means to make it nice. She still didn't understand what he did or why he had all the society connections, but it wasn't important to her. Every week without fail she would write to Rodney sharing her adventures and heartfelt expressions. He would return every one. Johnnie traveled a lot, and when he was home they enjoyed big, fancy parties and society events.

Of course, liquor was always involved in these outings, and it got so that Johnnie couldn't contain his jealousy for all the adoration and attention that Jasmine received from men and women alike. Sometimes they would come home with an extra lady or two. Jasmine was always thankful for these days. That way she and Johnnie could both be pleasured, and he wouldn't beat her for her continual rejection. He never hit her about the face, and mostly he would say mean and cruel things while breaking anything in his path. It was tiring and expensive for both of them.

Finally the day came that a producer was in town; he had a couple of burlesque shows in Paris. Mesmerized by Jasmine's pure beauty, he offered her a job doing what she loved. In less than a day she made her decision, packed her suitcase, and left Johnnie a note.

My love, our time has ended.

That was all it said. Johnnie's demise came swiftly from that note on. He'd been traveling, and upon his arrival the sinking feeling had already taken hold. Nobody really knows what happened after that, but it was rumored that his body was found in a remote, little clearing about thirty minutes from a train station somewhere in the South, with a gunshot to his head.

Vive la France! Paris was beautiful and Jasmine was eager for a new beginning. She only got a year's worth of time in Le Chat Noir before it ended, but that was enough time for some silent movie producers to take notice. Everyone was aware of Jasmine's ironic, wild, sexual abandon. She didn't mind showing everything, she loved to be pleasured by men and women, and she was just as good at giving as receiving; but she never allowed intercourse—ever. Everyone felt loved from watching her.

Jasmine Lilywhite made movies for approximately seven more years, secretly buying a farm in a remote part of Japan. She was famous for being known deeply by all her fans, but in truth she was never really known by anyone except for Rodney.

It was rumored that a mysterious, dark-skinned man arrived at her door one day, speaking perfect French. People like to ponder that it was Rodney Strong, the love of Jasmine's life and for whom she saved herself. They also say the couple moved to her secret farm in Japan so that they could have the life they always wanted. But for the most part, people don't usually know what they are talking about—and who are *they* anyway?

When we can recognize our place in the spiritual process we can better navigate it through understanding ourselves.

The Slayer's Path: Be Yourself

Learning to be yourself is one of the most important jobs you'll ever have in any life experience, and it begins with self-acceptance. No matter your condition or life circumstances, your job is to accept what they are; so that you may make informed choices about the changes you need to create a balanced life.

In this phase of personal spiritual development, your only real concern for what other people think and feel about you is to become aware of what you think and feel about yourself on deeper levels. Know that any judgment you hold about yourself will be presented through unearthing your hidden energetic patterns via the mirroring of others. This can often be a tumultuous or isolating time for your relationships because your dominant spiritual need is to focus on yourself first.

The best you can offer others at this time is your love, independence, truth, and honesty. But often it is those very things others find hurtful, as you may not consider the impact of your choices on them. Honesty becomes essential, because when you give all the information, your friends can make the right choice for themselves. Every person, at some point in his or her spiritual development, will go through this. This is the time to gird up your loins and move forward. A slayer will do this by developing their empathy.

Love at any cost

It's important to learn to discern a person's motivation; this discernment can be difficult to do when it doesn't occur to you what another person may be capable of. At seventeen, I met a man I really liked; he was twice my age. I would see him about town fairly often. Our conversations were getting longer and progressed into a mild flirtation. However, when it came to sex, I explained to him that I didn't have sex. I was saving my virginity until I got married. Somewhere in his small, reptilian brain he filed away the thought that I was lying to him. He kept things on a friendly level until my eighteenth birthday.

He bought me a birthday gift, a book entitled *Love* by Leo Buscaglia. On Sunday, the eighteenth of August, he invited me over in the morning to go for a quick workout and then lunch. When I got there he suggested that instead of going to the gym, we should make out for a while.

I thought, *What's the harm in that?*

Within minutes I was pinned down, and I couldn't move. While he was raping me, he said, "Oops, sorry."

My virginity was gone, just gone. And then after, he took me to lunch.

I'd not had sex before, and frankly I was only slightly sure that's what had happened. There was no physical pain, just the knotting anxiety in my throat and the immediate removal of my dignity and trust. The little seed of hate he left with me that day would grow up with my rage and become my bold, young, and virulent protector.

Afterwards, valiantly holding back the tears and still not completely understanding what just happened, I helped him straighten the bed, drove with him in his awful, smelly, old yellow truck to pick up his three-year-old daughter. When we came back to his place, I watched as he let her help him roll a joint. After he smoked it—me still with a lump of disbelief in my throat—we proceeded on to lunch. I have machine-gunned the facts because really the facts aren't very interesting at all. What is interesting is what came next.

The Slayer's Path: **Be Yourself**

Delusions are a girl's best friend

Bella Vista was a very popular eatery in Cedar Crest Village in the Sandia Mountains outside of my hometown of Albuquerque, New Mexico. It was born only a few years before me and was a local legend. It could hold hundreds of people at a time and produced all-you-can-eat chicken and fish for all of them.

I grew up thinking it was fancy dining as we couldn't afford to eat out much after my father died. Before he passed, our biggest excitement was the frozen chicken potpies we would get when my parents would go out to dinner at places like Bella Vista. They always dressed up, which lead me to believe it was an upscale restaurant.

Bella Vista was like a wood cabin on steroids with a beautiful view. So when Robby said we were going there for lunch I was a little beside myself. I had moderately tucked away the devastation of the morning's events, and now I was going to the deluxe Bella Vista for the first time with Robby and his three-year-old, just as the church crowds arrived.

There are only a few things I remember about Bella Vista. There were so many people I could barely breathe. I had a fake I.D. so I drank a whole lot of something alcoholic. As we ate Robby let his three-year-old run into every room in the place and didn't seem to worry or care. I realize that's not a shock, but it certainly was to me then. I let it go on for about twenty minutes, and then I got up to find her. I don't remember leaving or getting home, just collapsing on my own bed in the evening and crying until dawn.

Once the sun was up, I wasn't sure what to do. I told a friend who reacted like a celebration was in order.

Weeks went by and Robby wasn't calling. (I was hoping for some tangible, meaningful relationship, instead of what it was.) So I told another friend who, too, congratulated me on losing my virginity. Robby still wasn't calling, so I sent him a greeting card. Maybe it was a thank you for the lovely time at Bella Vista, but I think it may have been for Christmas.

Then a Godsend—I reached out to a different friend as a last ditch effort for reality and her response was: "It sounds like you were raped."

I was so relieved. "Yes, yes I was," I replied as the tears came.

Finally, someone had said it out loud.

New York City Is the Place You Oughta Be

Acknowledging the truth, I wasn't sure what to do. I didn't want to report it to the police for fear they would blame it on me. I was of age, and I did go to his house willingly. But I knew I had to do something. I couldn't let it stand as it was.

Finally, after about four or five months, he called. Again, he invited me to dinner, and we went to another legendary Albuquerque restaurant, Sadie's, where we guzzled pitchers of margaritas. I had driven to his place that night, so when we arrived back there, we were going to have *the talk*. We sat on the couch. I was drunk but feeling in control, and then *he* started to cry.

"Tracee, I am so sorry," he said.

"But why did you do it?"

"I don't know; I just thought you were lying to me."

> Know that any judgment you feel about yourself will be presented through the mirroring of your deeper dynamics via other people.

And then it happened. It just came out. With no warning whatsoever, I blurted through my tears, "But Robby, you can't do that. You can't do that to anyone else. They aren't as strong as me. Promise me you won't do that to anyone else."

As I looked into his crying blue eyes, he said, "I know, Tracee. I am sorry."

Well, that felt pretty complete. I got up, and said, "I gotta go."

After that conversation, I didn't touch another margarita for years. The seeds of hate and rage were beginning to cause me such anguish. I was bingeing often with these awful little frozen pizzas, crying at night because no one really knew the truth. The only time I had talked about it were the three conversations with friends I'd had right after it happened. Sleeping when I wasn't working was slightly helpful, until finally I got that demotion I'd been striving for.

I think the same week, the call came. A friend from high school was in college in New York City, and she needed a roommate. I quit my job the next day and started packing my things. My departure was quite sudden, and although the plan was to go for only three months, I packed everything I owned including my diploma, love notes from the seventh grade, and pillows. I loved my mom and my friends, but I knew in my heart that being in Albuquerque couldn't help me, so I left. I was on a mission to find the source of my pain. It seemed so much deeper than my experience with Robby. My reaction, as I found out through working with many victims over the years, was pretty common, but I knew there was more to uncover.

At the Milford Plaza

They say that someone who is willing to take you to the airport or help you move is a good friend, but the one who helps you move the bodies—they are a friend for life. I put pick-ups at John F. Kennedy Airport in the same category. After all, those boxes were kind of like dead bodies. I wondered what my friend thought as he waited at the gate and witnessed my arrival in a very modern Albuquerque outfit: torn up heels, straight-leg, turquoise cotton pants with an elastic waist band and a long tunic tank top of the same fabric, with a matching four-inch headband worn in fabulous *Flash Dance* fashion, with my hair all teased up and spilling over the top.

As we were taking the escalator to the baggage claim, almost home free, the escalator ate my heel. I still had a slight amount of pride and cared about appearances, so I left both shoes on and walked on tippy-toe so that no one would notice. We laughed all the way to baggage claim. Yes, Tom had quite a sense of humor, and it certainly came in handy that night, especially when we arrived.

I said, "There that one is mine, and that one, and that one, *and* that one."

My entire childhood was in those boxes. The only thing I didn't bring was my Baby Tender Love, which frankly, as of late, had not been very helpful or comforting so I left her behind.

Those boxes were heavy, but we managed to get them, and me on one heel, into the car and make it to the city. Tom definitely received the friend of the year award.

In Albuquerque during the 80s, for some reason they played a lot of commercials for the Milford Plaza, the historic hotel in the heart of Broadway. I remember the jingle with the catchy tune about what a privilege it was to stay at the Milford. Perception is everything so on the first night I arrived in New York City, after picking me up, Tom carted me and my four ridiculously large, coffin-sized boxes containing every single thing I owned to the Milford Plaza Hotel. *Oh my, things were really turning around,* I thought. It was a beautiful entrance, and I do believe they still had bellmen to help with the boxes.

The room was smaller than I'd ever seen. It had its 1940s charm left over from the actual 40s, dirt and all. I didn't care; I was in NYC! It didn't bother me that there was just enough room to walk around the 1960s bed without hitting my knees on the wall, nor that my four massive boxes had to be stacked, and left just enough space to wiggle through the bathroom door.

That is one of the few nights I remember quite vividly. My life had already been changed forever, twice, but this time something new and profound was happening. The great divide between my head and my heart was cracking open. In New York City, I would meet many other people like me. I wasn't leaving my home, I was coming to it.

PEACE HAS COME—BUT THE *FOUR HORSEMEN* WILL STILL RAVAGE HUMANITY—STIRRING UNREST IN THE WORLD—UNTIL ALL HATRED IS DEAD AND ONLY LOVE REIGNS IN THE HEART OF MANKIND.

The Four Horsemen of the Apocalypse (1921)

The Slayer's Motto: Good to Know

A slayer must know how to continually move forward and when it is time to do so. They must have all the facts, or recognize when there may be vital information missing, but still move forward. The slayer's motto is, *Good to know,* just for this reason.

For example: "You've just won the Lotto!" *Hmmm, good to know.*

"Someone just ran into your car and totaled it." *Hmmm, good to know.*

Learning to respond instead of react is a slayer's strongest tool in times of trouble or joy. Remember, the devil just wants to catch you off guard, and when you are in deep times of profound transition it is easy to be caught off balance during an emotional reaction.

At this point in your development, you've let go of what you don't need, so you can't react in the old way. But you're not yet sure of the direction you're going, therefore unsure of the appropriate new responses. A neutral stance is needed.

Hmmm, good to know.

It is this neutral stance in turbulent times that will, over time, help your brain begin to produce a more calming chemical cocktail and more balanced emotional responses. The more harshly we react to something, the more likely it is we've been caught off guard by the circumstance or situation. Remember, the devil wants you to stay insecure or in your confusion as long as possible.

The Devil Wants You Needy

What relationships look like through self-acceptance

If you are in any way confused about yourself, just about everyone you invite into your life is going to have an opinion about how you live it. Ultimately in life we have to do two things: be accountable for our actions and learn to trust our instincts. There are times to lean on your own understanding and then there are times to lean on the understanding of others all the while being radically honest with everyone. The process of self-acceptance is learning to trust yourself and your relationship with the Creator.

Relationships during this time can be precarious. If you have friendships in your life that in the past have been based on need, sometimes transitioning them to a relationship of equality is difficult. A friend's well-meaning attempt to school you on what you need to do may be more of a burden than a help. If you're inundated with everyone else's needs for you, it can obscure your awareness of what you need for yourself and your complete healing. This phase is precarious because the great equalizer is tender yet definitive honesty, communicated to yourself first and then to everyone with a vested interest in you. It's a real temptation to want to walk away from uncomfortable situations, but your best action is to dig deep and be honest.

The Slayer's Motto: **Good to Know**

Communication with neutrality

Transitioning a relationship of need to one of equality means that no one is to blame, but everyone is responsible for their contribution to the connection. You either like the choices someone makes or you don't; allow yourself to communicate honestly and set boundaries without guilt, anger, or hurt. The presence of those emotions indicate areas where you may be resisting self-acceptance.

Inevitably, moving forward means maturing to a place of independence in trusting yourself and your relationship to the Creator. Trust means that ultimately we are prepared and willing to deal with the consequences of our actions. When this is the case, it doesn't mean you don't make mistakes; it means that your mistakes are yours. Your responsibility is to process through the consequences, sometimes on your own without the help of friends and loved ones.

Over time, leaning on friends can take a toll on them and the relationship you have with them. People want to be there when you are first going through a crisis, but the tenth time you're having the same crisis they may be less interested. If you find yourself in the same situation, repeatedly, with the same unwanted consequences, there is a deeper pattern going on.

This is life. It takes time for us to become aware of ourselves on all levels, so repetition is necessary. However, if you do nothing about it, then you put your friends and loved ones in the position of enabling your unfortunate choices. It is continually valuable to recognize that we and our relationships are changing all of the time. Learning to discuss those changes and to set new boundaries and parameters for the relationship is mandatory.

I've worked with many married couples who run into trouble a few years down the road in their marriage because of the beliefs that they brought into the union: our love is deep, sacred, and will last forever and ever unchanging. The illusion of becoming one with another human being is a bit of a fantasy. I am not saying that marriage doesn't inspire a unity that is unlike other relationships. But that unity is based on the knowledge that each individual must experience their own personal spiritual integration. Until you've done it yourself, you certainly can't do it with another. So until that time, each individual in a union must learn to be accepting of what they and their partner must go through individually first and together, second.

Sacred marriage

Unification between the spiritual and the physical, or the Creator and humanity, is the true concept of marriage. The idea of marriage between a man and a woman is, in fact, a spiritual one: the Creator, the divine masculine, entering into the physical body, the divine feminine. The Star of David is the symbol that represents this phenomenon, with the divine sword entering the sacred chalice, unifying and creating true spiritual marriage.

In the East, the Tantric image of the *shatkona*, a six-pointed star, communicates a similar idea of spiritual marriage. So, the only possible sacred marriage is between you and your Creator. Anything else is a contract. Sacred marriage is the process that every soul seeks, and the process brings us around to the experience of faith. As you can well imagine, it takes a great amount of preparation for a physical body to receive the energy vibration of the Creator. The practice of Tantra is in fact a meditative practice that helps to cultivate one's energetic self-mastery.

> Trust means that ultimately we are prepared and willing to deal with the consequences of our actions. When this is the case, it doesn't mean you don't make mistakes; it means that your mistakes are yours.

The endocrine system in the body goes through a series of awakenings (due to the path of the *kundalini*) that opens up our energy body to higher frequencies. As we open up to higher frequencies, our other bodies or energy layers (like the emotional body and mental body) must adjust to incorporate the more subtle energy. The emotional body grieves in order to shift, and the mental body needs more wisdom in order to adjust. Going through such an energy shift often promotes consistent emotionalism and anxiety until the energy bodies and physical body balance out.

The soul is the vehicle that drives this process for every individual. It is the information, or set of imprints, contained in the soul that gives us tools and a starting point of experience from which we draw our current life events and perspectives. Each experience draws to us more of the same until we hit a point of critical mass. When we do that, we have the opportunity to make a different choice that heralds a different result. If we continue to make the same choices, then we continue to suffer in those choices until enough neurological circuits are changed, allowing us finally to make another choice.

The Slayer's Pact: Never Run

It is a common reactive response to cut bait and run in the face of uncomfortable changes in a relationship. A slayer stays in the situation and chooses to communicate, finding a way to express their truth with humor and kindness. Letting someone you care about know what you need in your connection is owning your place as an equal in that relationship. However, centering your focus on providing for your own needs allows your relationships to evolve past a connection based on necessity, opening you to true authentic and loving unions with all of your relations.

The 50/50 rule

The operating rule of thumb as the burgeoning independence grows inside of you, and ultimately in your associations, is called the 50/50 Rule. It's the understanding that everything you encounter on every level—from thoughts, feelings, experiences, and events—is somehow connected to you, and you contribute half of their purpose. The idea is that you need the way things are happening in your life at any given time, as do the people with whom you participate. The intensity with which you speak to someone is a direct result of their density and vice versa.

If you find that people are often yelling at you, then ask yourself what you're resistant to hearing. What do you, or the person you are engaging with, get out of the event or circumstance? Know that this growing independence you're experiencing is leading you away from feeling victimized or being victimized in any way. If you are a victim then you attract perpetrators, and if you're a predator you attract victims. If you are to take complete responsibility, then you must expect it from others, leaving you neither as a victim or a perpetrator. This is a principle, of the degree of healing that comes long after blame, accountability, and forgiveness.

From this perspective every chain of events looks different. If you've been victimized, then this perspective comes after processing your grief and anger, once you've been able to forgive yourself and all others for the events or circumstances you've experienced.

The spiritual process to how we heal

The most important question to ask yourself is how you can take responsibility for your part in this world dynamic? This is a matter of spirit. It's common to make the assumption that spiritual matters are religious matters. They are not one in the same. Religion is the ritual that aligns us with our spirit and our relationship with God; it is not the relationship itself.

Religion is much like a radio, which only transmits the vibration of sound, but is not the sound itself. In order for all of us to progress, we must acknowledge ourselves as energetic beings. It is unnecessary—but helpful—to be religious, and we are all spiritual. We must acknowledge that our physical body is very dense energy. As the frequency becomes higher, the energy patterns become faster, more powerful, and more subtle; not slower, less powerful, or less subtle. Our energy body, emotions, and thoughts are all forms of matter, which are propelled by the faster frequencies of energy that preceded them. As we integrate and heal old patterns we must go to the origin of the formation of matter, which is in spirit.

> If you take complete responsibility, then you must expect it from others, leaving you neither as a victim or a perpetrator.

Why people don't heal

In general, people don't go back to the origin of an issue because we've been conditioned to treat the symptoms and cover up the problem. We are taught to fear what we are not familiar with and are sometimes unable to accept that the origin of an issue lies in a place we cannot directly recall.

Let's look at the origin of fear. Without attempting to rewrite the creation story or contradict any religious theory, it is important to look at the function of fear and for a moment to embrace the concept that fear is a tool that assists us staying in our physical body, keeping our body intact, and keeping our spirit attached to our body in this reality. If you can embrace this concept just for a moment, then you can have a glimpse of understanding why fear is so popular and important. With this new wisdom we can begin to conceptualize what it would be like to create the tools necessary to live without fear and what the possible results would be.

Choosing to live

Choice is the first tool to master. It begins with the concept that the consciousness of every human being is made of a higher self, middle self, and lower self. In this model the higher self is the highest frequency to which we have access. The middle self is the cognizant mind, and the lower self is all of the energy that is contained in our spirit.

When the cognizant mind decides to do something, it makes its request to the higher self, but prior to success it scans all the information in the spirit or lower self to see if the energy seeking to manifest matches the lowest frequency of the souls energy. All focus will then move to that lowest common denominator of the energy to decide whether or not certain concepts or belief systems are too dense to be able to manifest the cognizant desire. We then are subject to choice. We now know what belief systems we have in place that are not in alignment with what we want, and we can choose to give them up and adopt new ones that match our goals.

The Slayer's Pact: **Never Run**

The importance of your environment

Your home and your body are your sacred space. There may be times in our lives when we don't have the authority to decide with whom we live or even what we put in our body, but eventually as you grow and mature you must learn to be accountable for what you ingest and who you choose to have in your life.

Sometimes when we are seeking peace in our lives, we must let go of grief or anger in order to create a space for the peace to reside. If we are looking for a new job or seeking to lose weight, then maybe we must leave behind old self-doubts or the things that reinforce them. Either way there is a trade-off, letting go of one thing in order to create space for another. If you find during this phase that creating distance between you and those you love is necessary, then remember: a slayer doesn't rely on fear or cruelty.

A slayer always takes responsibility for their choices; if you need time and space from a loved one or acquaintance it's because of who you are, not who they are. You may not like their choices and express such a sentiment, but your goal isn't to judge or criticize. Your goal is to be clear and not leave them hanging in a vulnerable state waiting to reconnect with you. I am not speaking about being dishonest nor about just being nice. Not making a clean and open break keeps a psychic cord between you and your loved one that remains open and draws energy from both parties until it is shut down completely for both people. You see, getting away from someone isn't always actually *getting away*. Sometimes, separation only amplifies your connection to what you don't like or are uncomfortable with about them, until the situation becomes clearly and openly resolved in the physical world for both people.

> DOES IT BRING YOU PAINFUL OR PLEASURABLE EMOTIONS? IT IS BEAUTIFUL; IT IS PROFOUND; IT IS DEEP. TO ME THE PAINFUL AND PLEASURABLE ARE BLENDED IN THE BEAUTY, AND I THINK THE TWO MAY BE ONE.
>
> CLARENCE DARROW

Surrender to a broken heart

Surrender is the phase of spiritual process that acknowledges a release of old patterns, persons, places, or things. This phase promotes a surrender to the discomfort or lack of understanding of what will be taking its place. Surrender at its height is a broken heart; or as I like to think of it, the heart opening wider. We live in a culture and world that encourages us to run from the heart breaking, and as you know, that just isn't an option. The very way our spirit teaches our bodies to expand and adapt is through pain and heartbreak of some sort. The heart breaking is the most beautiful experience you can have, and most people don't even get to enjoy it.

We are taught that emotional expression is weakness, which—if you have to experience it—is best kept private. My mother was about forty-five with three tweens and teenagers when my father died. The day of his funeral and that first Christmas after his death I caught her crying. I remember thinking exactly that: I *caught* her crying. It is culturally supported that we appease or stop a crying child, rather than teach them that life and growth is a series of heart expansions and that one can manage those experiences. Absolutely some people need to cry more than others, but expressing what we call grief does not imply being in a weakened state: it is a process of strengthening into wisdom, originating from the spiritual realm, and entering into the heart, mind, and body.

The idea of karma

Karma, a Sanskrit word, is a Hindu concept referring to the idea that for every action there is an equal and opposing reaction. It includes—but is not limited to—the spiritual concept of duality: good and evil, light and dark, yang and yin. Karma is not simply the idea that if you do something bad, something bad will happen to you. It means if you kill someone, with that comes the complete and total understanding—or burden—of its impact. This understanding does not come in what we consider to be linear time and space; it is its own dimension of time and space that we humans may relate to as a past life.

What we call a burden, is actually unexpressed grief from a previous time passed down through birth to future generations that may be better equipped to process it. So that means we are currently sitting with the burden of our spirit, our ancestors, and the collective. It's easy to see why some people cry a lot.

Weakness is receptivity

It is through what we consider weakness that we access the subtle energy bodies. Weakness, then, is receptivity, and receptivity is an ultra-sensory perception of anything not physical. I am not going to deny that in caveman days it may not have been conducive to survival that you collapse to your knees in wailing grief as the saber-toothed tiger approaches to eat your family. It may be best to buck up and run.

Today, however, there are few circumstances where survival depends on the reigning in or non-expression of emotion. Those people in those circumstances will eventually get to it in one life or another. Receptivity is the way that the Creator sends down its wisdom. So an open mind with a closed heart leads to insanity, like King Solomon in the Bible, and a closed mind with an open heart leads to self-pity and persecution like maybe Marilyn Monroe.

When I use the word *closed*, it is figurative. No part of us is ever literally closed; we may just be limited in knowledge or experience in some way. The process of surrender opens us to releasing what limits us, whether it is an idea, person, place, or thing.

Most of all go with courage and keep your humor knowing that whatever you may find; it is infinitely better to have found it.

Accept defeat

Defeat, in this context, is total surrender. I am speaking of defeat as an emotion. When we feel defeated, we have arrived at the beginning of our destination for that cycle of experience. The game changer for me was when I realized what it meant to surrender to my higher self and to know what was about to arrive was going to be better than I could imagine. The very reason you are surrendering is to open the way to the part of yourself that can see everything, to expand beyond your current limited vision.

Feeling defeated is certainly cause for celebration, but not for a party. For our addicted friends out there, this is the phase that is the most difficult. If you are so inclined, then this time breeds the desire to escape the pain of acceptance and reach out for something to alter your relationship to it. Drugs, alcohol, cigarettes, sex, food, or shopping won't change the pain in anyway, nor will it make it disappear. It will only change your relationship to it for a short period of time, until you are dropped back down into the pain and sorely less equipped to handle it because now you have added another layer to the burden. This is where the addict takes a wrong turn every time. Until we are truly willing to accept defeat and allow our hearts to open in the painful way that they do, we cannot move forward in ourselves or with others.

Honesty

The first step to complete surrender is to be totally honest with yourself. Redundant, I know, but the mind and ego do not always want to admit what the heart and the self know. Accept that you did not get the job, he or she isn't coming back, the relationship has changed and nobody wants to fix it, what happened to you really happened, you're poor, you're sad, you're hungry, you feel ugly—whatever it is, accept it.

Once you accept it, you become empowered in it. You cannot change something that you won't acknowledge. The affirmation I use during this phase is: *I accept myself completely and fully on all levels. My world is exactly as it should be and I am grateful.*

Stinging words to utter when you feel devastated, I know. Think of them as the tunnel out of hell. If you will just walk through it, then the most auspicious path is already laid out for you, the one path that will bring you exactly what you need next—whether it be courage, peace, joy, cash, or companionship. Trust that there is a space deep inside of your heart where this information lies dormant, and the act of grief activates this knowledge and attracts to you exactly what you need. You don't even have to go out and get it. If you will create a space for it, it will come. This leads us back to the brain again. When we cry for ten minutes or more, the neurons in our brain change. It is like we erase the ugly stuff so that we can replace it with good stuff. Yes, this is an over simplification, but it's absolutely true in its essence.

> CONSCIENCE IS THE MOST SACRED THING AMONG MEN. EVERY MAN HAS WITHIN HIM A STILL SMALL VOICE, WHICH TELLS HIM THAT NOTHING ON EARTH CAN OBLIGE HIM TO BELIEVE THAT WHICH HE DOES NOT BELIEVE.
>
> NAPOLEON BONAPARTE

How I Met Jasmine Lilywhite

One night I had a dream. I was sitting in a small, dark, private movie screening room. I was by myself, sitting in the center chair looking at the old, roll-down white screen they had in my youth. The movie began to roll; it was a silent film, dark and grainy. A stunningly beautiful yet approachable woman appeared on the screen. The movie was in black and white, but somehow I could sense the actual colors of her clothing.

Her hair was in a short, platinum conk hairdo, and she was wearing a frilly bustier that cupped just underneath her completely bare breasts, with a peplum ruffled skirt that wasn't more than a foot in length and open in the front. She was dancing on a burlesque stage, using her chair as a prop, when she flipped around the front of the chair to face the audience, sitting and oh-so-gently swinging her legs around in a full straddle, pantyless for the world to see. I sat up in bed gasping for air, and knew that was me. It was me.

After an adrenaline rush and good laugh, it all started to make sense. All sorts of memories started coming to mind. Just days before, I'd been to the local copy shop where one of the young male clerks asked his co-worker if I was a porn star. While this was the first time (that I know of) where someone had just come out and said it, others have always had an unreasonable fascination with my sexuality, from having an uninformed opinion of it to being fascinated with my physical body—mainly my breasts.

One day in NYC, from the time I left the house until the time I reached back home, everyone had commentary on my breasts: men and women alike, people I knew and those I didn't. At first I felt defeated, and then it made me laugh. The absurdity of it: *every* person that day had taken notice and said so.

I have memories of being in kindergarten and little boys trying to pinch my bottom. As I grew to be an older child, on at least ten occasions I had run-ins with perverted men asking to see my genitals or wanting to show me theirs or just saying nasty things to me. I was never physically harmed, and I always ran. Upon telling an adult, a few times the police were called, but none of the predators were ever captured. I have to say that at the time, it was looked at with less interest than it is today. I am thankful the awareness is so different now.

While I was never hurt in the physical process, it did leave me with a lot of confusion about how and why people responded to me as they did. From earliest ages, I was very clear on my stance about not having sex and had no problem setting those boundaries. However, because I was a highly empathetic child I was highly sexualized— by that I mean I had a lot of charisma—and people seemed to respond to it. A second chakra mojo: from as early as the age of five or six I had a sexual awareness of my body. I had many boyfriends in the tween years and a few dates in high school, but didn't have sex with any of them, and they always seemed surprised at my clear voice and conviction about saying no to any kind of sex. I didn't mind the kissing though.

After having been raped as a virgin, it only brought out the pain I'd felt my whole life and amplified my need for self-control. In fact, it didn't make sense to me how others could be so easily led into things they didn't want. I expected that all girls had the thoughts and experiences that I did. Living in my first New York City apartment up near Columbia University, I was ready for an experiment. It seems that after the rape, I shut down my emotional self in hopes of a glimmer of self-preservation.

I was a cashier at the now famous Tom's Diner, featured in the TV show *Seinfeld*. My weight had shot up to about two hundred pounds, and I was constantly being hit on by Pete the manager. A customer who came into the diner several times a week seemed to really have an interest in me. His name was Lucien. He was French-born and lived in the neighborhood. I found him intriguing because he wore an entirely black leather outfit with silver studs and spikes, including a billed hat, pants, boots and jacket, with a smorgasbord of silver jewelry, but he didn't ride a motorcycle. I'd only seen folks who ride with that sort of gear.

Every week Lucien would come into the diner and flirt with me. Finally, I suppose after a few weeks of sizing me up, he asked me out. We went for a drink in the neighborhood on a couple of occasions. He was mildly interesting, but I didn't feel anything. He was very good-looking and sexually appealing, but I still didn't understand why his clothing choices got my attention the most.

After about a month of little outings, he invited me over to his house. He said he wanted to cook me dinner. I'd considered that sex would be a part of the evening, but really couldn't conceive of the route the night would take. I arrived at the appointed time. I was unaware that he lived with his sister. She was home, so we went immediately to his bedroom. Evidently, there was no dinner made either.

It was a fairly large apartment on 105th Street. His room was sparsely dressed with a twin bed and two chairs: a large, wingback chair, which faced a small, metal folding chair. He walked over and sat in the wingback and motioned for me to sit in the folding chair. Now, all of the hairs were standing up on the back of my head. I didn't feel unsafe, but I knew that this is what I'd come for. He began to speak...or *something* began to speak.

He began to criticize and berate me, saying incredibly silly things like other men probably didn't want me and only he did. I was amazed. I then had a flash of understanding: he was trying to make me feel bad about myself so I would sleep with him? But it didn't make any sense at all. Did he really think he'd be successful?

It wasn't just that. There was something else. Everything he'd said and done since I'd met him was all designed for this moment. Even the illusion that sitting in the larger chair made him more important was part of the plot. Now *that* sort of conviction made me feel a little sexy.

It was a unique dichotomy to see what an unfortunate, disgusting human he was and still be impressed by all the work he put into this moment. What I didn't consciously understand in those moments, but on some level was familiar to me, was that he was portraying traditional dominant behavior. I suppose, maybe it would have made more sense if he'd just handed me a dog collar and called it a day. But then what fun would that have been?

I kept up my funny barbs as the responses to his ridiculous statements and questions. All night we sat there in a battle of wills. It was at least four in the morning when I allowed him to have sex with me. I really needed to know if I would feel something. I didn't. I laid there for what was truly the longest two minutes of my life. It seemed to drag on, and I still didn't feel anything except for a little disgust. Once done, he rolled over and fell asleep.

I couldn't stay there with him. I nudged him to walk me to the door and had to chuckle when he told me I could walk myself there. Shaking my head, I got up and got out. This was my first walk of shame, walking home in the middle of the night from what was certain to be a one-night stand. I didn't have the money for a cab ride home, which was about ten blocks up.

> Trust that there is a space deep inside of your heart where this information lies dormant, and the act of grief activates this knowledge and attracts to you exactly what you need. You don't even have to go out and get it. If you will create a space for it, it will come.

And then it happened. I burst into tears and what followed shocked me. The rage seemed to come from the depth of my soul up through my feet encompassing my entire being. I screamed at the top of my lungs and darted up Broadway running as fast as I could until I reached my door. I was filled with such rage and anger I didn't know what to do with it all. The months of stasis had finally been moved. But I wasn't quite prepared for the force. It was finally time to do the battle for my own lost soul, and I knew this was the beginning.

Lucien called me for months after that, but I'd gotten what I came for: the piece of myself that had been so deeply submerged that I thought I'd lost it. It was my power. From that point on things changed. I lost weight and I gained honesty. And life, while still difficult on so many levels, became fluid and acquired meaning. Everything had meaning. And, unfortunately, Lucien didn't find the submissive he was looking for in me.

Loving yourself

To love yourself means to bring love into every situation by being accountable to yourself for what you go through, giving it meaning through seeking its deepest wisdom. Yes, while I certainly could have avoided going through the Lucien situation, having that experience was the beginning of a major healing transformation for me at the deepest level.

It's easy to focus on all his flaws, his obvious agenda, and the dominant/submissive scenario he set up for me. But more importantly, his flaws exist because of his pain and anguish, as did mine. Lucien and I met at our lowest common denominator. I needed him to be exactly who he was so that I could excavate my way to the deepest source of my soul's rage. This understanding allowed me to have no bitterness or attachment to him on any level. At the end, there is only love.

Reinstating self-trust

The process of change for me in forgiving the man who raped me, and ultimately myself, was deciding I no longer wanted to live using anger as my protection. Anger could no longer be the instrument to my survival because it was diminishing in every way. Somewhere inside I knew that if I were to give it up, I'd have to truly resolve my rape with the man who raped me, and reinstate my self-trust. How was I going to do that?

The year of transition was rocky at best. I moved to Los Angeles and lived in my truck and on the couches of two very generous friends. Living and finding work wasn't easily navigated for me. It took me months just to find something part-time and an apartment. It was a year before I began to make new friends who were consistent and had similar values. I had three jobs, including a full-time position as a restaurant manager. It was truly the beginning of a new way of life for me. I still nurture a few of the relationships from that time.

One night, we all stayed after work to have a couple of drinks. We drank, laughed, and chatted for several hours. I think it was the most fun I'd had in a year. Finally, I felt marginally safe and even a little happy. And then it struck me: now was the time. I was going to call Robby and confront him and this time it wasn't going to be about what he had done to me. No, I was going to confront him about all the suffering I went through because of what he did to me. I needed him to know how much I'd suffered.

I valiantly walked over to the payphone and dialed 411 and got his phone number. I couldn't believe he was actually listed. I laughed. And then I called; it was about 2:30 a.m. his time when his machine picked up.

All I could think to say was, "This is Tracee Dunblazier, and you need to call me back."

I strolled back over to the bar where my friends were and announced what I'd done. One jaw dropped at a time. Maybe it was a bigger deal than I'd realized.

Back at home, I'd just settled down when the phone rang. I knew it was him as I answered. We stayed on the phone for almost two hours and I said everything I needed to, but somehow still didn't feel resolved. *Maybe I need to see him*, I thought. And there were the words, coming right out of my mouth.

"I need to see you." I couldn't believe I was saying it.

Next thing I knew he responded, "Okay, I will come out to see you. I'll call you in the morning with my plans."

The next day he called with the day and time. He told me that he'd never traveled outside of Albuquerque so he was a little nervous, but he really wanted to help me resolve things. The day and time arrived and I'd gone to the restaurant to wait for his phone call, and by *wait*, I mean he was to leave a message on my machine at home and I'd call and retrieve it, and then we'd meet.

The hours passed one into another; he was at least three hours late. I checked several times, and no message. Finally, I left the comfort of my friends and went home, to the glaring red light of the machine. There were three messages. The first one saying he'd arrived, the second asking where I was, and the third saying, "Wow, you really got me back. I come all the way out here and you blow me off. Well, I'm going home now; I hope you feel better."

I had to laugh. I couldn't have planned this. Why had none of those messages come up when I called to check? I felt a little bad for him, but not really. I'd spent my entire day waiting for him, too; I just couldn't believe that all of this happened. I'd always known our relationship was karmic on many levels.

About a year later, I went back to Albuquerque to visit my mom. Again the feeling came over me to see him. At this point, I wasn't quite sure what there was left to resolve, but there was something. *Maybe I just need to physically see him*, I thought. So about an hour after I called there he was at my doorstep.

Whoa...there *it* was.

The first realization: he looked like a lizard to me. He had morphed into something else, and maybe it's what I had perceived all along. We left my house and he suggested that his family was having a barbeque and we should go.

Hmmm, this was interesting, he wanted to take me to meet his family? We arrived about thirty minutes later after a fairly quiet and moderately uncomfortable ride there.

Upon our arrival it looked like it had been a big production several hours before and now there were only a few adults and a gaggle of kids running around. No food, no drinks, just a huge backyard with empty tables and chairs, and a volleyball net. Robby went to play volleyball with a couple of the men there, and I sat down to watch. This was getting stranger by the minute. About fifteen minutes later, Robby came over and sat next to me on the steps of the back patio.

He said, "I really am sorry, Tracee. I wish there was something I could do to make it up to you, How about dinner and a movie?"

We both burst out laughing. I think that was the funniest thing I'd ever heard, and it was laden with the truth. There was absolutely nothing he could do, and he knew that. *Now* it was finished. We waved good-bye to his family and left. Finally I felt triumphant and at peace.

From that moment on, I never looked back.

The Slayer's Ritual: Burden Transformation Protocol

Call it out. Remember: you own it. It doesn't own you. The burden you carry is yours, even if it is amplified by someone else's energy or by an entity. Call the burden to the forefront of your awareness.

Name it. Naming what ails you is the first step to transforming it and everything you have created because of it. The burden of your making must ultimately be the burden of your choosing. Once you name it, you have brought it into the physical realm where you hold the power.

Get the vitals. Everything we have has come from somewhere. You must always find out who, what, why, when, where, and how of the origin to what ails you. Once you get all of the information in your cognizant mind, you will naturally begin a new point of view and most likely begin a grief process. Grieving releases all of the emotional energy you have attached to the situation.

Heal it. Binding a demon or banishing it from your life only saves it for later. Your goal here is to heal it, forgive it, and transform it. When it no longer is what it was, it cannot attach to you or hurt you any further because the dynamic no longer exists. This is a good time to call in angelic or ascended master assistance. Jesus, St. Michael, Mary, Krishna, Chong Koi, Quan Yin, and the Buddha are all perfect to help release yourself of otherworldly entities. Ask for the unwanted energy to be removed, and identify the place in your physical body where you've been holding the energy or entity. Ask for the energy or entity being removed to be transformed into usable energy for the universe or to be sent back to the dimension it came from.

Replace it. Removing and transforming energy leaves a void in your spirit that must be filled with a new, higher frequency energy. A bad habit must be usurped by a good one. I use the visualization of colors and sentiment to fill the empty space. For example, if you are afflicted with a *tail*, call on St. Michael to assist you in its removal. Follow the protocol: call it out, name it, get the vitals, and then heal it. Ask yourself to show you where it is connected in your body, and ask St. Michael to remove it. Then fill the space with the sentiment of truth, peace, and love or anything else that feels appropriate. Ask yourself which color best resonates with those sentiments, and then visualize that color being poured from the Creator down through the top of your head into the space where the old energy had residence. Now, make an altar of gratitude.

The Slayer's Altar: Gratitude

What you will need:

- Green or White candle
- Tobacco or cornmeal for an offering of gratitude
- A handwritten prayer or love letter to yourself

PART FIVE

SPEAK UP!

You Can Be Demon Free

The Slayer's Weapons:

Eternity, Conviction, Understanding,
Faith, Peace, Resurrection, Dignity

The Story of John and Adele Battle

The weathered, wood door was most notable for its beautiful stained glass window. It was John's work. John was the love of my life, or should I say, the only real love I knew in my life. It was Natchez, Mississippi, in 1852. John Battle and me—I'm his wife Adele—we lived in the little overseer's quarters on a good-sized plantation called Red Grove in North Adams County; we were both free blacks in profoundly complicated and unpredictable times.

BEAMS OF HEAVEN, AS I GO,
THROUGH THIS WILDERNESS BELOW,
GUIDE MY FEET IN PEACEFUL WAYS, TURN MY MIDNIGHTS INTO DAYS.
WHEN IN THE DARKNESS I WOULD GROPE,
FAITH ALWAYS SEES A STAR OF HOPE,
AND SOON FROM ALL LIFE'S GRIEF AND DANGER,
I SHALL BE FREE SOMEDAY.

CHARLES A. TINDLEY

The new state of Mississippi didn't really like the idea of freedmen and after 1820 used every venue they could to ensure difficulty for the approximately 460 freedmen who were in residence, with everything from arrests for vagrancy (which carried outlandish sentences) to new legislation and the implementation of exorbitant fees to acquire and renew their free papers. In fact, freedmen had to continually prove their status with these papers and being found without them could result in being sold right back into the slave trade.

I was born a slave in Northern Virginia. The rape I'd endured at age twelve filled me with rage. I screamed and cried quite a bit after that until the beating I received shut down any desire I had to speak. I could speak, I just didn't; they just assumed I was broken. But I was a good listener. They liked to keep me in the house as I never spoke back, which afforded me an education of sorts. People will speak freely when they are not reminded of your intelligence.

Now let me tell you about Mary, the unofficial owner of Red Grove. Mary Battle was a proud woman and feisty, she usually got her way in most situations. Until Mary came along, the Battle family hadn't been too controversial. Her daddy and his daddy before him had owned slaves, and in their minds they had been fair. But somehow when Mary was born in 1770, the tide of clarity and vision began to transform the family—at least for the decision makers of the Battle Estate. Yes, from what I understand, because of Mary, things began to change. Mary said that slavery didn't make sense, that there was enough for everyone, and that the fear of not having enough just makes your spirit small. It leaves you disconnected from the very thing that can get you everything you need.

It was rumored that Mary's father had been a part of the Underground Railroad, and Red Grove had harbored many visitors over the years, some of whom stayed. Mary's father had also freed all of his slaves many years before and had given them options to stay and create a life within his business. So many of them did, including John, who'd been born at Red Grove like his father before him. They'd been given the Battle name and been with the Battles for three generations now.

Mary's Papaw was enamored with her from the moment she was born. And as she grew into a strong, young woman, most importantly she had his ear. She was fiercely loyal to those she respected. Mary was the youngest of five children, and even though she got along just fine with her siblings, they were all much older and thankful for her presence because it meant they could leave. All of them, except one, had a great disdain for the South and got out of Mississippi as soon as they were able. Two older brothers had gone to New York, and a sister had married and moved west. The only sibling Mary had close was a brother who'd just died at the privileged age of ninety-five.

> But God's grace has always been with me.
>
> Adele Battle

Mary was left with the entire plantation and all the businesses and properties therein, and her brother's death would have to be kept secret. The only people who had property rights at the time were white men. Neither women nor blacks could yet legally own property, but it would only be a matter of time. The deeds would have to remain in Bolger Battle III's name until things changed. They had a small, quiet funeral and buried him in the family plot on the east end of the property and no one spoke of it.

Johnson's Red Winter apple was God's grace of the Red Grove plantation as it bloomed late in the season and brought fruit until the end of October and early November, ensuring food for the winter and sometimes all the way to summer. It wasn't known for its flavor, but its thick, deep-muted red skin and flattened shape kept it fresh for months. The other crops of the farm had seen better years, and Mary had entrusted her apples to the best man for the job: my husband. John was the overseer of Red Grove and the reason the apples had always done so well.

Red Grove was quite a spread, and although she didn't act her age at all Mary was getting on in years. She was glad to have John there to help her manage it. The 485 acres carried multiple crops—including quite a prolific apple orchard and several structures. It was those apples that gave the plantation its name.

John and I were soon to celebrate our tenth wedding anniversary. Even though our marriage wasn't respected by the state, Mary wanted to give us a beautiful wedding to renew our commitment to one another, and that's just what she did. We had two young children and worked so hard every day of our lives; she really wanted something beautiful for us. Maybe somehow she felt guilty about what was coming, I don't know. Mary told me once that she knew the moment she saw John lay eyes on me that we'd be together. In fact, he saw me long before I ever noticed him.

I was nineteen when I came to Red Grove. I'd been separated from or lost all the people I'd known in life. The family I was born to labeled me as violent, emotional, and just too much to handle. Then I'd come down with the fever and taken ill. They considered me a throw away. By the time I arrived at Red Grove I was sick and unable to function. My owners just left me on the side of the road, half-dead, on their move out west. Just by chance a friend of Bolger Jr.'s found me and brought me straight to Red Grove, knowing that Mary would take care of me. By all accounts I really shouldn't have survived all that turmoil. But God's grace has always been with me.

It took me some time to recover from my illness and acclimate to where I was. No one had ever been this kind to me, and it took some time to learn and trust my new surroundings. The years went by and I became comfortable with my life, my quarters, and my job helping Mary, who had taken to me almost like kin, almost like a mother to a daughter. Although I never completely believed it, I appreciated the effort.

One day Mary asked me to bring some lemonade and snacks down to John at the cottage on the orchard. It was harvest time and she knew John didn't always eat well when it was busy. I thought it was strange, but did as I was asked. When I arrived, I found John taking a break and mulling over some paperwork on the porch of the cottage. I saw the light beaming from his smile as I walked up. I knew why Mary had sent me. I felt the warmth of his light in my heart. My mind, however, was a different story. I didn't trust Mary and knew she had something up her sleeve. Could it really be my happiness? My mind was fierce and it'd take some time to accept the inevitable.

John and I were together from that day on, at least in spirit. Within two years' time we jumped the broom. I moved into the cottage with John, at Mary's encouragement of course. Mary didn't think she needed twenty-four-hour-a-day help anymore, just regular hours would be fine. Most of all, Mary knew that John and I needed each other and said no one deserved to experience the love of a family more than we did—even if it would only be for a little while.

> We danced and sang and for a moment, we forgot where we were. We were happy.
>
> Adele Battle

Mary's family had been a part of Natchez since the beginning, and because of that they claimed respect from the locals. They ran a profitable business and brought a lot to the community even though they never really abided by the social mores of the time. They were just powerful enough to have their ways overlooked. People ignored the rumors as best they could but probably not for much longer.

It appeared that Mary Battle had a few enemies, especially a militia that had just been formed by three young white boys who had a reputation for bullying. The youngest was twenty-three. They supposedly had political goals and backing, but we all knew what that meant. Everyone in town knew her brother Bolger III had taken ill and it was only a matter of time. That militia wanted Red Grove.

Mary felt the tide turning; she didn't know exactly what was happening, but she did know that she wasn't long for this world and when she was gone, there'd be no one left to legally take over Red Grove. She'd put John Battle in her last will and testament but couldn't file it with anyone. She knew even if the laws changed by then, the state would still fight it. The same as if they knew Bolger III was gone. Yes, Mary knew change was coming and it would get worse before it got better.

On this day, however, there was going to be a beautiful wedding. We chose an enchanting spot all the way to the north of the orchard where a little stream ran through near a clearing of trees. We built an altar and decorated it together in order to lay our vows to God and each other upon it. We even celebrated with rings that Mary had made. I think those rings may have just been the beginning of the end.

All the folks at Red Grove were heading over to the clearing now. The September blooms had taken over the entire orchard and with the sun blazing at the two o'clock hour, the perfume in the air was almost syrupy. The food tables had been set out and were quickly being filled by the contributions of all of our friends and neighbors. Mary provided everything else along with the most beautiful cake and liqueur for a special toast. This was a big event for everyone including Mary. It was the largest event held at Red Grove since her daddy died, and there would be more food than anyone could finish. Only a few people from the town were invited; it wasn't safe for the word to get out.

That was by far the happiest day I'd seen at Red Grove. We danced and sang and for a moment, we forgot where we were. We were happy.

I took John's hand and said, "*You* make me happy."

I still remember Mary's toast. "To young hearts so eager and full of each other, embrace and love one another every minute that you have to do so—tonight has been promised to you." Her words struck me and stayed with me the rest of the evening.

It was about one in the morning, and we'd just gone to bed when I heard some rustling outside. In a few moments I saw a couple of lanterns out the window. John got up and went to the porch. It was those militia boys.

I heard some loud voices and arguing and then John shouted, "What are you doing?!"

And just as I got to the door John was gone, and they were pulling me out of the house across the porch, and dragging me down the stairs by my hair. Before I could gasp for breath the noose was on my neck and I was strung up to the hundred-year-old magnolia that shaded the cottage. My spirit was free from my body. Soon John found me and our spirits cleaved to one another. I heard they got Mary too.

> AS WE LEARN TO CONFRONT THE TRUE CAUSES OF OUR DISCOMFORT (OUR ARCHETYPAL WOUNDS), REDEFINE THEIR CULTURAL CONTEXTS, AND EMBRACE THEIR HEALING FIELDS, WE MUST ALSO MOURN THE END OF A FAMILIAR IF HARMFUL COMPANIONSHIP—OUR AVOIDANCE MECHANISM. ONLY THEN CAN WE FILL THAT VACUUM WITH THE DIGNITY FIELDS THAT HAVE LONG BESTED THE DARKEST SIDE OF OUR HUMAN TRIBAL JOURNEYS.
>
> DR. MARIO MARTINEZ, THE MINDBODY CODE: HOW TO CHANGE THE BELIEFS THAT LIMIT YOUR HEALTH, LONGEVITY, AND SUCCESS

The Slayer's Path: A Broader Viewpoint

Demons want you to feel small and to be small. They want to make sure you have the most limited view possible of all things. They want you to remember only pain, anguish, fear, and trepidation. They want you to believe that your destiny lies in your DNA, that you are relegated to the same sufferings your ancestors had before you and that you can trust no one.

Change begins with the dignity that only you can give yourself. You can't get it from your family, your culture, your race, or your religion, nor from your political party, your job, colleagues, or boss, nor from your mate, friends, or children—just you. You have been enriched by your Creator and made from the essence of dignity: all you have to do is embrace and embody that dignity.

We do this through our worthiness. It is the kind of worthiness that determines what you do or don't deserve, but not because you *deserve* it. The context: you attract things because you are prepared to receive them. You have become suitable to sustain that dignity.

A forty-ounce pitcher is only worthy of five eight-ounce glasses of water. In order to be *worthy* of more water, you must get another or larger pitcher, which requires additional preparation. In order for you to be worthy of higher-minded concepts like dignity or equality, for example, you must eliminate the idea of separatism, fear, or lack through transformation into the ideas of integration, love, and abundance—ideas that ultimately hold more water.

People react out of fear because they are afraid of losing something: themselves or their means, their freedom or their power. Until they're able to access another possibility and dignify their reactions, they will continue to feel enormous fear generated by their mind, body, or spirit in order to stay safe.

Feeling this fear leaves them open to bias and bigoted feelings towards those whom they feel threatened by in some way, whether that threat is ancestral, spiritual, mental, emotional, or physical. The reality is that you can't possibly have enough bias to keep you safe from everything and everyone.

A slayer knows the only thing that will keep them safe is to be openhearted and present in every situation and see things as they are, and not as he fears they are. That way, if things happen to be unfortunate or scary, he's able to address them with precision and mastery and to make the most optimum decision possible.

Carrying the dead: the way our past affects our present

Carrying the dead is the way that we hold onto unresolved energy in our lives, everything from ungrieved loss and bad decisions to ancestral curses and entities from other dimensions called upon by you in times of need. Fear and other strong emotions that go unchanged can be carried with your spirit across time and space as well. These other emotions include ambition, anger, gratitude, grief, hope, humiliation, love, power, and powerlessness, to name a few. As in the case of colors, there are primary emotions that are the foundation of all other feelings.

This unresolved energy is not limited by time or space and stays with a soul until the energy is transformed by recognizing it in the physical reality and then changing it to another form. The process of grief is a way that we change energy from one form to another. The action of crying actually changes the way the brain tells the body how to relate to such traumas or events—by changing the neurons in the brain. The action of grief changes our feelings, and the action of mourning changes our behavior.

The Slayer's Path: **A Broader Viewpoint**

You always have access to all that you need

Now that we've worked out the whole self-esteem issue. Remember, self-esteem is not necessarily how you feel about yourself but the nature of thought patterns and habits that you exhibit daily. From your thoughts and habits, you formulate a relationship to yourself and others.

When you are born and for a time afterwards, your thought patterns and habits will come from your spirit and the way you are nurtured by your caretakers and environment. A lot of people have this idea that an infant is free of inclinations and that who you are is something you accumulate from birth, but it is not the case.

You already arrive as a complete package. As you get older you will begin to include the responses or reactions you glean from other people as well. I describe it this way: to deconstruct something you must have an understanding of how it was put together in the first place. At some point in your life, you will need to take apart an aspect of yourself, not because you are less than or broken but because the thought pattern or habit has worn out its usefulness to your evolution.

> In order for you to be worthy of higher-minded concepts like dignity or equality, for example, you must eliminate the idea of separatism, fear, or lack through transformation into the ideas of integration, love, and abundance.

Bring God here

Why are we evolving? I like to think of it as a little game of *bring as much God here as you can*. Back in the olden days, a few thousand years ago, people used to think about God as being something outside or separate from them. Religion was created to practice the idea of communication the Creator. Then we considered through our practice that Divinity is manifest and working in the physical world. Through spending lifetimes in worship of God outside of us, we realized that the Divine is within us, and maybe we are God in human form, meaning there is no separation.

We are of the essence of Great Spirit. Keep in mind here that all of these thought patterns are a way to cultivate a perception of yourself and Spirit that can be useful in your evolution. Perceiving yourself as God is not meant as an excuse to be an arrogant, power-seeking jerk who thinks they are better than anyone else. If you do, you're still in the evolutionary spin of ten thousand years ago when we believed that God would smite us down like bugs if we didn't sacrifice our neighbor or a goat.

The Slayer's Motto: Heartache is Heart Opening

Depression is the new black

I'd like to take a moment to revisit the idea of depression and its spiritual value. In our culture today, some folks have really gotten diagnosis-happy. If they cannot withstand their 24/7 lifestyle, they want a pill to fix it.

Our mind, body, and spirit already have ways of processing information that is beneficial to each and every one of us individually, if we will only learn to pay attention to the subtle language that our subconscious speaks to us. Our spirit knows everything we need and exactly how we can get it.

I will, at this time throw in a little disclaimer: I am not anti-Western medicine or anti-anything for that matter. I do believe it is imperative that we recognize the wellness of every part of ourselves and which includes spirit. Our soul is our driving force, beyond all other things.

Yet culturally we do not have a pervasive non-religious education about mental and spiritual health, or help for those without a diagnosis. There is a consistently budding new age community constantly pumping out information that needs the respect of the medical community in order to glean an expanded following. When there is a wider audience, there will definitely be fewer medical diagnoses. And I suspect there may be some folk who don't want that. I know the devil doesn't.

> Hate builds walls and separations from love in order to limit understanding and promote singular comprehension of an aspect to how things are. Love disintegrates those walls and promotes the expansion of our vision to the Truth of the way things are.

Nature's way of self reflection

Just as anger and adrenaline constitute nature's way of helping you become hyper-alert to your surroundings to keep you safe, depression is the spiritual mechanism that helps you to self-reflect. Depression happens when you are energetically overloaded and need to take time to reflect, express, and process unexplored emotion. It allows you the time and space to recognize any of your thought patterns that are no longer necessary for your continued development.

For example, let's say you have somewhere in your spirit the story of distrust. You don't ask for help because your main belief is that you won't get it. You then always complain you have no help and end up repelling the people around you who could give you help. When someone tries to give you assistance, either it's not good enough or you believe there is an ulterior motive because the message in your spirit says that you should trust no one. Thus, you don't get the support you need, you are tired, overworked, under appreciated, and inevitably you get depressed and eventually sick. Well, that doesn't sound like a lot of fun, does it?

When you begin the process of depression, it comes in stages. It begins with subtle adrenaline rushes and crashes that leave you tired. Maybe you catch a flu virus that gives you the opportunity to explore your feelings. But you take some medicine or vitamins and power through it, not stopping, not reflecting, not paying attention to your needs—or making sure they're met.

Of course, you can't, because deep down, you cannot trust anyone to help you and there is *always* too much to do. Your next stop on that train is to continue this pattern over and over again, possibly for years.

The brain at this point has a physiological makeup that expresses this pattern and consistently tells your body and mind how tired you are. This is when other beliefs like *I am not good enough, Nobody loves me, Why is this happening to me?* and *I don't deserve this* are able to creep into the experience. *Ah ha*—you are depressed.

Severe depression takes a long time to cultivate. So, congratulations! If you are there, you've been working hard and the upside is that you are good at something and have achieved success in your goal.

Subtle depression exists for long periods of time and goes unnoticed and unaddressed long before severe, debilitating depression takes hold, at which point intervention of some sort is necessary. Oftentimes, people become aware of their depression when it hits a tipping point through some form of calamity: they get in a car accident, are mugged, lose a friend or relative, go into collections or foreclosure, lose a job, or possibly suffer from a natural disaster.

Anything traumatic can tip them over into not being able to function and manage their daily lives. But make no mistake about it: it takes a long time of consistent spiritual imbalance to cultivate the physical body into physiological patterns that promote depression.

Again, the good news is, once you understand how something was put together, it can be taken apart piece by piece and rebuilt however you'd like. It takes work to change thoughts, mind frames, and habits—but it is *all* possible.

It's not all black and white

For almost forty years of my life, I've had the privilege of a very unique perspective, culturally and racially speaking: what it's like to be perceived as a white woman and live with the feelings of a black man and woman in our country. Until I was at least thirty-five, I didn't really see, feel, or experience what others saw or expected when they looked at me.

I'd always been immersed in the emotion and experiences, on a subconscious level, with the spirits of John and Adele. I had unconscious culturalisms of the African American Slave experience that would reveal themselves through my responses to certain things. For example: knowing the racist roots of the nursery rhyme, "Eenie, meenie, minie mo." Yet, having never had any exposure to its origins in this life. Throughout my life many people, black and white, have said things like, "You really do have a 'black' thing going on," or, "They [black people] really do seem to take to you," or, "You're the blackest white person I know."

Although my usual immediate response was to cringe a little at peoples need to differentiate and create racial separation, we'd usually just laugh and move on with the conversation. I didn't always know what I'd said or done to get that response. But, on some level it made sense to me.

Couldn't *they* see what was going on? In my spirit, I knew I carried many souls and felt their feelings, experiences, and sentiments as my own. I understood, from birth, the presence of the racial divides that are experienced, definitely here in America, from all sides. Why couldn't other people? I thought daily that I couldn't be the only person with this experience.

> IT IS THE STILLEST WORDS WHICH BRING THE STORM. THOUGHTS THAT COME WITH DOVES' FOOTSTEPS GUIDE THE WORLD.
>
> FRIEDRICH NIETZSCHE

Kudos to my parents

My parents really did give me the best world I could've had to grow up in. Don't get me wrong, there was no extra money, there was no pedigree of brilliance, and they weren't necessarily activists for any certain cause. No, the world they gave me was filled with truth and honesty, humor, and a work ethic. I wasn't steeped in the bigoted, fearful, or righteous opinions of the sixties and seventies that I knew existed elsewhere in my community, and that I understood both of my parents struggled to overcome while growing up.

My direct community as a child consisted of predominantly white, Hispanic, and Native American people, with probably less than thirty black or Asian folk. The only thing my mother said to me about racism was, "Tracee, you'll need to understand that not everyone sees things as you do." That certainly wasn't the sentiment I experienced from many of the parents of my friends'.

As a young girl of twelve, I remember thinking, *Wow, Mom, good on you, for not trying to put on me what I know was put on you.* I was referring to the, *It's common so it's okay* or *It's how I grew up* justification for racist sentiments I saw in many places around me.

As it regarded racism, I knew it was her way of acknowledging what was, as of yet, still unspoken in me. What I was unable to articulate at the time was that there is only one race on this planet, the human race.

While I've always been aware of the insight I carried, insight that was well beyond my years, it has been my path to cultivate a voice, one that wasn't given at birth, one that speaks in simple, honest terms about the parts of humanity that continually get swept under the rug, like racism, sexism, and bigotry. If I wasn't allowed to ignore them, how could I let others?

The Slayer's Motto: **Heartache is Heart Opening**

To be clear: color is not ethnicity

I'm not saying on any level that I know the day-to-day experience of being a black man or woman in the United States, in the twenty-first century. I do not. To be exact: My ethnic make-up goes like this; 63% Great Britain, 19% Western European, 9% Irish, and 9% of Spanish/French, European Jewish, Italian/Greek, and Finish/Russian.

While it is valuable to have ethnic pride it is unacceptable to hold ethnic hate. In my experience, my spiritual leanings far outweigh my DNA. I understand from every vantage: being enslaved and the path to freedom that begins with the spiritual and emotional healing of the experiences of our ancestors of every lineage.

Trust me, through my struggle to understand the many levels of spiritual experience I hold and to begin to communicate it, I have met many people who were offended, enraged, and dismissive of me and my notions.

I've felt their anger and rage like an arrow to my heart. Luckily for me I had no fear of it, only a tender heart with tears to transform their pain. It has been through those exchanges that the Creator transformed my pain and revealed to me my purpose.

What I've learned about acceptance and compassion

I now understand that I don't have a complete understanding of what other white women may experience being white or a woman; that while we will experience similar spiritual dynamics, no two people have the same experiences ever.

There are entire communities, cultures, and countries that carry with them ungrieved and sometimes unacknowledged pain. Perpetrators of bigotry, ignorance, and hate are expressing the preliminary stages of their spiritual process and lack an understanding of the magnitude of the power of love and the unlimited love to which we all have access.

Hate builds walls and separations from love in order to limit understanding and promote singular comprehension of an aspect to *how* things are. Love disintegrates those walls and promotes the expansion of our vision to the Truth of the *way* things are.

Many have died with that pain in tow and it then is carried into the future generations either with their spirit or the spirits of their descendants. Pain is never forgotten, it is only transformed. And, the form it takes is up to you in every choice you make.

There is no antidote for bigotry as those with fear and pain will always find a way to express it. It is only through the giving of compassion to another in pain that we are irrevocably changed. You can't unknow love once you've experienced it, and unfortunately there are some who don't know love.

The only way to respond to ignorant people is with unequivocal faith and a consistent compassionate voice, knowing that you will always have what you need in all ways at all times. A crystal clear voice expressing who you are and an undeniable joy in the privilege of wielding the power of truth in all you do. In the face of that, ignorance residing within the ignorant does not stand a chance.

No judgment here: but you're a racist

Look, it's a hard pill to swallow as you begin to excavate the deeply held secrets of your habits and fears. And, fear is a habit, one intended to keep you alive, but a habit nonetheless. Learning to uncover, disintegrate, and recreate your world view is profound and inevitable. Of course, I am not just speaking here of racism but of any form of preconceived ideas or assumptions you make about another human being based on any other time but the present moment.

Doing this leaves you in a weakened state and vulnerable to conflict or calamity, not to mention embarrassment, humiliation, or even a missed, shining opportunity. When you are not present in an empowered moment you will be less effective and essentially disempower yourself. Nobody wants that.

How to hit a moving target

Bigotry is a moving target. You've got to focus on where it's going not where it is. This means if you feel like someone's views of you are limited then ask them, with compassion. It doesn't serve anyone to expect people—no matter which side of the coin they're on—to just *get over it*. People are bigoted for many varying reasons: because they've been abused, because it's what they were taught, because they were born with the inclination in their spirit, because they are fearful, because they are an insecure human—I could seriously go on for days. But at the end of the day, it doesn't matter why they are. The power lies in your ability to wield your compassion with the accuracy of a stealth bomber. Compassion in the face of another's pain and fear is the only way. Compassion can, and must, be discovered, cultivated, and practiced.

Whew, now that I got that preach out, I'd like to tell you a little story.

One sunny Sunday afternoon I was driving out of my apartment building when I noticed a police car at the entrance/exit. I didn't pay it any mind. As I slowed to look both ways before driving out, they were on me. I don't know if I can describe what happened well enough to truly do it justice.

But, all of a sudden (with shock and awe), both police officers went into high alert mode, the officer to the back right of my car drew his gun on me and the female officer approached my car door, slapping it and yelling, *"Get out of the car!"*

And then both of them in unison, *"Get out of the car!"* several more times.

I sat there stunned and confused with my hands at ten and two on the steering wheel. As I'm sure was the point. The officers were making so much racket, that it left me paralyzed just long enough to recognize that the shock was turning into rage inside my body.

In that moment I completely understood why some people just lose their minds and rebel, and consequently people die. And in *my* specific situation, all of that angst was generated by the police officers, and it wasn't good or to me seemingly necessary either.

What I found myself doing in the midst of the crisis was slowing my breath and speaking in a firm quiet tone: "I am not the one," over and over. I had my hands up. I don't remember who opened the door, and as soon as I was out of the car I was bent over another car being frisked. Still slowly in a firm quiet tone saying, "I am not the one you're looking for."

In those moments, I didn't know that the other tenant at the building who drove the same vehicle as I did had a female lover who socked her in the face and then stole her car. The police thought I was her.

I can't speak to the way our police force is trained and to its efficacy, but I know how I was able to handle that situation on that day, ensured my safety in what could have been a profoundly unfortunate situation. I don't know if *these* two officers were deliberate and following their training, but luckily because of my training I was calm in spite of the strife they were creating. This ultimately is the purpose of training: to remain calm in spite of the adrenaline that pumps in high-octane situations.

The minute they saw me *these* two became wound up. Any situation will always fall to the lowest common denominator, and I was not accepting the one I was being offered from them. Now, I certainly couldn't say the same for the rage-filled Tracee of twenty years ago. Dealing with my own emotional mastery has taken me decades of practice.

As I think about it today, I have an immense gratitude for having had this experience. I am fascinated at the cosmic alignment of events that led to it, and the valuable insight I was gifted because of it.

Educating our warrior force in laws of spirit

I have a deep love and reverence for the police, emergency personnel, and armed forces. I've had glimpses of the profound trauma many first responders, officers and soldiers witness on a daily basis, the immense strength, courage, and bravery they must muster up in every moment. And, for some warriors, the danger is their life.

I am sure there are many that understand the distinct difference between power and force, the former being a spiritual energy that can encompass and transform all things and the latter being the energy that seeks to match or surpass its opponent. And from the news headlines, I know there are some who do not.

What I do know: you cannot invite warriors into hell without the proper spiritual training and then expect them to win every spiritual battle they enter on another's behalf, especially the mental and emotional battles of bigotry, racism, and all forms of gender inequality that are so deeply rooted in our history and humanity.

These courageous men and women that protect us end up fighting for their souls long after the physical battle has ended. I believe this generation of warriors deserves to use the knowledge of the twenty-first century weapons: energy, compassion, telepathy, and presence in addition to their weaponry.

The Slayer's Motto: All Things Will be Made Right

I learned today that there is a difference between healing and restoration: healing is the process of bringing into balance what has been out of balance, while restoration is the process of being brought back to your original perfection. Transpersonal empathy is empathy you feel for those you've never met. Most often it is in times of tragedy that we experience it.

Indeed, when there is a great loss of life or property there is an energetic realignment happening for the planet and her inhabitants. In no way can it be considered punishment for sentiment, behavior, or people but only recognized as a spiritual transformation agreed upon, spiritually, by those affected. Keep in mind here that purpose is not a justification for bad things to happen, but only a recognition that there is a greater good at work. When you ask yourself or the Creator why awful things happen, please consider the broader purpose that the loss of such privileged souls support and the service that those who process emotion for others, provide.

The journey to St. Joseph's

The night began with happy hour on the balcony at the Maison Dupuy on Toulouse and Burgundy. Always at the finish of a trip to Baton

Rouge, we celebrate and relax with an overnight stay at a haunted New Orleans hotel or Plantation somewhere on the river road hoping to facilitate some spiritual healing for the land and her buildings.

Even though I was quite tired from the previous week or two of work, my commitment to heal the land and deliver lost souls was usually pretty high. This trip I had the privilege of an entire day of rest and was well stocked with energy *and* inspiration.

Before arriving in New Orleans this trip, I had a burning question. I asked the Creator about Bourbon Street. I'd always skipped over the many invitations to go and really didn't understand the nature of the darkness there and why it existed, aside from the obvious Marti Gras shenanigans that go on there every year and the inevitable excess of many party goers. (This kind of activity can leave quite a spiritual imprint on the land and in buildings.) My answer came as the evening progressed.

After a beautiful dinner at Muriel's Jackson Square with my dear friend Faith and her brother Scott, we decided to take a stroll down Bourbon Street.

> There is a difference between healing and restoration: healing is the process of bringing into balance what has been out of balance, while restoration is the process of being brought back to your original perfection.

I've avoided the Bourbon Street stroll for the eight years I've been going to New Orleans. Something about the unhindered drinking and debauchery it's known for has always felt taxing for me to witness. Also, it's really, really loud.

My friend's and I agreed at Royal Street that tonight was the Bourbon Street night. Of course, they'd always been willing, it was me that was the hold out. But tonight I felt especially prepared and guided for whatever we may find. I wanted an answer to my question.

We headed down Bienville to Bourbon. Bourbon Street certainly was a feast for the senses, albeit a bit of a rotting feast. The sounds and smells were as I suspected: loud and penetrating, the slight smell of urine wafting up after every dark corner. At around St. Peter Street we ran into the nicest, funniest, crewmen all dressed in black. They were the greeters for a bar called the Krazy Korner.

Their job is to charm you into the club with the blaring band and it's hoped that you'll take advantage of one of the many drink specials—this night it happened to be three for one—no kidding, three drinks for the price of one. We moseyed in and on up to the bar, and wouldn't you know, they didn't have one of the three drinks we ordered. No harm, no foul.

We wondered back out, keeping a close eye on some of the regulars of the street and of the completely drunk and unaware tourists who visit on any given night. There was a worn-hard (but not quite put-away wet) blonde girl who couldn't stand up straight looking as if she were negotiating her next fix from the overeager young man making awkward pelvic thrusts at her as she giggled and took comfort in the sturdiness of the wall that was holding her up.

Down the road a piece there was another young lady wearing Daisy Dukes and some sort of fragile top, which she kept pulling up to reveal the tattoo that began somewhere under her shorts and continued up her belly. The conflict she had with keeping her top on seemed as if it may have been only the beginning of her troubles. The gentlemen on the street didn't seem to mind.

As we walked, I was drawn over to the other side of the street where an equally loud band was playing rhythm and blues. As I stood outside, a young man was sitting in the passenger seat of a small van covered with a decal of four scantily clad women of many ethnicities baking edibles and rolling joints.

He said, "Hey, have some edibles."

"Hmmm," I said, "I definitely don't need any, but thank you."

Somehow the conversation moved from his mobile marijuana business to the topic of God. He asked what God I worshipped, and I told him that I thought we all shared the same one.

"Oh, you're a monotheist. I am a polytheist. The God I worship is goals over distraction."

I told him that was a pretty good philosophy and to keep up the good work. I wondered into the bar with the R&B band. Who knew what little pearls of devastation we were about to find? The song that drew us in was "The Love Train."

People all over the world, join hands, and board the love train, the love train.

As we were standing there, a young lady backed her bum right into my friend Faith. The girl didn't look much over twenty-one, with a fresh little face, short red hair, and enormous cleavage that she appeared to sport as part of the job. She was the Jell-O shot girl who made a living seducing folks into taking a shot of liquor-filled Jell-O from the container she held in her mouth. I guess that the fanny backup was the beginning of the seduction.

Both Faith and I turned down her offering, and as she backed up to the lady next to us, we noticed that she had about a month left in her pregnancy and looked as if she could deliver any day. As my heart wrenched, I turned my attention to the band on stage, a group of seriously seasoned professionals who had at least forty years in the business and treated the performance like it was their daily workout, all the while not missing a beat. They were absolutely mesmerizing. The two lead singers were wearing second skin red shirts with pleated white pants and red belts as snazzy as they must have been in the 1980s. They were truly the guardians of the musical heart and spirit of Bourbon Street.

We wondered out to the street again. I heard the dulcet tones of a man's voice singing next door. I walked over to see that it was a woman playing the drums and singing; she called herself the Gypsy Lady, something or other. I don't quite remember. The picture on the board she used to advertise her gifts must have been taken in her heyday several decades ago. So to see her still holding it down on Bourbon Street with her baritone voice was quite impressive.

I couldn't decide if still working in such an unforgiving environment such as Bourbon Street was a testament to their career longevity and integrity or just bad luck. They all seemed to be glad for the work so who was I to question it?

The night was coming to an end as we headed back to the hotel about six blocks away. It was well after midnight, and all the streets leading to Toulouse and Burgundy were quiet. We crossed the paths of a man enjoying a snack on his way home, as well as one of the Bourbon Street regulars who seemed to be so inebriated that he followed us for a few blocks until he finally asked if we knew of a place he could poop.

Fortunately, or unfortunately, we did not and we continued one more block to our destination, arriving safely. I laid down, so tired and ready for sleep, but alas sleep would not come and the real work would soon begin.

It was around 1:30 a.m. as I drifted off to sleep. Faith was still awake and working on the computer. I think I fell asleep for a few minutes, but soon became aware of people running and screaming as if in total panic. I awoke thinking it was a terrible dream and turned over on to my other side hoping the terror would abate. As I closed my eyes I felt an enormous fear, a terrible heaviness and sadness, penetrating the depths of my spirit.

I felt many sad souls now standing around me, hoping for some relief, in addition to the demons there to do the devil's bidding by keeping those devastated souls in this place.

> The land has memory. It holds deeply and in a sacred place all that it has witnessed.

All the while, this continuous movie ran in the background, with people running screaming and yelling, "Fire! Fire!" Flames and smoke were everywhere. Roofs were going up in flames and falling unceremoniously to the ground.

Now I sat up shaking my head. I was aware of all of my physical senses, and there was no one screaming and no fire anywhere but still I could feel their terror and grief. For a few moments, I felt scared. I then felt the touch of the angel Zadkiel on my right shoulder reminding me to pray. I laid back down, closed my eyes, and called on the angelic reinforcements that are always at my disposal.

I called on St. Michael, St. Raphael, Chamuel, and Uriel. Now I was clear on what was happening. I'd asked, earlier in the night, how Bourbon Street got to be the way it was. Now I had my answer.

The land has memory. It holds all it has witnessed—multiple holograms of pain and desperation layered one on top of another like a broken record playing over and over again for anyone who will listen—deeply and in a sacred place. In addition, there were restless souls unable to vacate the earth plane, held in bondage by the demons seeking to feed on their desperation and fear. Layers of lies and betrayal, multiple attempts to prove whose God was the strongest, led this land and all who have dwelled upon it to suffer in their illusions that we were separate from our Creator, illusions that until now had not been forgotten or healed.

Now it was time and I was the conduit. I was the physical-world connection meant to moderate the healing the Creator had sent down at this time and in this place. As many times as I've done this, I am amazed at how quickly I get drawn into the pain of others through my empathy and for a brief moment forget my life.

I called on Michael to surround these earthbound souls with his light and love and deliver them to their oversoul. I called on Raphael to send down his golden light to infiltrate and obliterate darkness, fear, and confusion in every corner of the city. I called on Uriel to erase the memory of what appeared to be a great fire, to put it out once and for all and erase it from the spiritual database. I called on Zadkiel to keep my prayers focused and strong; and finally I called on Jesus to stand with me, collect every demon, and remove them from this dimension eternally by transforming them back to love. Finally, I fell asleep.

The day journey soon began.

I woke up maybe an hour or two later. I did not want to awaken, but I knew I would never get restful sleep with such a powerful night on my mind. I didn't completely remember all of the images of the rapture that took place, but I needed to begin the work to understand them.

The Slayer's Motto: **All Things Will be Made Right**

I Googled *Great Fire of New Orleans*. Called the Good Friday Fire in the news clippings, it happened on March 21, 1788, and took out the area from Toulouse and Burgundy (where I was staying) almost to the waterfront. One of the few buildings it didn't ravage was the Convent of St. Ursuline. Of the information I found, it appears that only one person lost their life that night, but from what I witnessed many people lost a part of their souls.

The devastation was complete with a total property loss. They spent six years rebuilding only to be ravaged a second time in 1794 with another fire. It was at this point that most of the French architecture was lost. The Spaniards, who had taken over, began to rebuild much of the property in Spanish style using brick, stone, and iron in hopes of thwarting the power of any future fires.

Faith and I got up and set out on the beautiful, sunny morning, walking down the street near where we'd dined the night before in Jackson Square now in search of breakfast. It seemed the likely choice as it wasn't too far away, just a straight shot down Toulouse to Royal St.

Both of us seemingly sure of where we were going. We walked and walked until finally we realized that directly in front of us was the Convent of St. Ursuline. Several blocks past where we'd intended to go. The area seemed familiar. Maybe the place we were going was just a few blocks to the right, we decided. A little perplexed, as we thought we'd backtracked our steps from the night previous, we were certain to be near our destination.

We kept walking. The convent was nowhere near where we'd been the night before, but in fact, it was just beyond the perimeter of the 1788 Good Friday Fire. When we finally got to Jackson Square, we arrived at St. James Church, which happened to be the western perimeter of the fire.

After breakfast we decided to go to the church and light candles as a final ritual for all those who suffered, reenacting the layers of spiritual pain this city had been laden with.

As I lit eleven candles for them, a woman standing next to me began telling me what a beautiful church they had at the Convent of St. Ursuline. It was gracefully exquisite and more amazing than any she'd ever seen.

"Today it was a special celebration for St. Joseph's Day, one of the few days of the year they opened the chapel to the public."

She cheerfully recommended we go.

As we were divinely guided, we continued walking the southern perimeter of the Good Friday Fire and ended at the celebration for St. Joseph at the St. Ursuline Convent. We were given food and lucky fava beans in honor of Jesus's father the carpenter, who is the Catholic saint for helping the destitute and suffering.

A beautiful journey of St. Joseph indeed.

On the plane ride home that miraculous St. Joseph's Day, March 19th, I sat between a nun and a Baptist. It was a good day.

> IT IS A MATTER OF EXPERIENCE THAT IN OUR MOMENTS OF DEEP EMOTION, TRANSITORY THOUGH THEY BE, WE PLUNGE DEEPER INTO THE REALITY OF THINGS THAN WE CAN HOPE TO DO IN HOURS OF THE MOST BRILLIANT ARGUMENT.
>
> EVELYN UNDERHILL

The holy death

Many spiritual philosophies hold the concept of the *holy death*, which is a death or completion of the spirit. When death occurs in any situation it marks the end of one dynamic and the beginning of a new one. If we acknowledge that all things are created of spirit than spirit would be the place to go to make changes to those creations.

I had a friend once, Andrew, who had been born and raised in New York City. By the age of twenty-seven he had lived a life of difficulty: drugs, alcohol, isolation, and abuse were all a part of his sphere of experience. Finally, he started to recognize that even though his abuse was not his fault or begun by him, he was doing a fine job continuing the abuse by the many choices in his life.

Thus began his holy death.

Andrew was a smoker, had been for years, and to remind himself of his daily choice for self-abuse he kept a fifty-gallon, clear Hefty bag full of his empty cigarette packages—hundreds of empty cigarette packages—in his bedroom across from his bed. If you've never been to NYC, the apartments you see on television aren't really how most people are living; oftentimes a New York City apartment is really small. This clear plastic bag took up so much space that you could not move anywhere in the room without having to cross its path directly.

I remember walking into his room and seeing it for the first time. The air was thick and the energy stifling. I sat on the bed and wept. In that moment, I understood Andrew's divine courage to look at his life and at himself and to sit in his choices. He no longer relegated himself to being a victim. He slept every night in the honest presence of his choices. I know you might find it sad and just plain horrible, but in truth it was a real victory. For the first time Andrew had the opportunity to take personal responsibility and look at the things he could control, his personal choices.

The beginning of that process is called the holy death. The process begins with the loss of innocence and the acceptance of responsibility. When we begin to understand and embrace change, we can begin to recognize the consistency of the new pattern that may allow us the freedom of surrendering to the flow of the universe and to our individual success. Most of all, go with courage and keep your humor, knowing that whatever you may find, it is infinitely better to have found it.

Andrew and I had sparse contact over the next few years. The last connection before the end, Andrew showed me how he was now cutting himself with his freshly made scars. One of the many ways he was trying to tolerate and express his pain. He'd also gotten into shooting heroin and cocaine. I'd never known him to do drugs, but he told me the girl he was with wanted to document his drug use on film.

What the hell was going on with him? I thought.

It was maybe another year after that visit when I ran into Andrew on the street somewhere. He lived on the Lower East Side, and as we were chatting I realized that the next night I had to work at the jazz club until two or three in the morning and then had a five a.m. call for a music video; right around the corner from where he lived.

"Hey," I said, "Would you mind if I crashed at your house tomorrow night?"

"Sure. Just give me a call."

And call I did the following night (or morning) around one-thirty a.m. When I arrived at his house he seemed jumbled, nervous, and upset. He asked if I had any money he could borrow. All I had was the twenty dollars I'd made at the bar.

I gave it to him, and he was out the door. I had a very bad feeling. I walked into his bedroom, and hanging over his bed was a life-size cutout of a very lovely woman. As I walked closer I was shocked that she looked just like a classier version of me; it was a very elegant photo (evidently she was a fashion model) and she was wearing a black dress with her hair up in a bun. I just couldn't get over how similar our faces were and that he had this foam cutout of her hanging over his bed. I knew it was significant, but I didn't know why.

Maybe within fifteen minutes I fell asleep and was soon awakened by Andrew's arrival. I heard the door open and looked to see him staring at me through the slightly open door. But more noticeable to me was the immense, dense darkness that shrouded him. It was an energy that was at least ten feet in circumference around him. I felt a pang of fear reverberate through my body.

"Andrew, are you okay?"

He paused for a moment, "You know, Tracee, I think I've really done it this time."

"I don't understand. Come in, and sit down. What do you mean?"

"No, no, you don't worry about it. Go back to sleep."

"Andrew, I see that something is wrong. Tell me what it is."

He stayed at the door. "You know how I always find a way to sabotage things? Well, I think I've really done it this time. I don't think I'm going to get out of this one."

At this point I was up and walking toward the door when he said, "Don't worry about it, Tracee. It'll be fine. Just go back to sleep and I'll call you tomorrow."

My heart was aching. "Are you sure?"

"Yes, I'll call you first thing." And, then he was gone.

I believe only one person saw him again after that; the person that murdered him.

Two days later, I received a phone call from a woman who said she was his girlfriend. She asked me if I'd seen Andrew, and I had not. She told me no one had seen him since that night. He was missing.

I told her about our conversation and that I was worried for him. She and I decided to meet the following week for a coffee. In walked the lady in the cutout. It was strange sitting in her presence, and as she told me about all the things they'd been into, I couldn't help wondering why I was called into his life in the last of his moments. It obviously wasn't to help him. He was missing.

This girl was like a dog with a bone, and thank goodness. Unbeknownst to us, Andrew had turned up in the East River and was buried in New York's potter's field, a cemetery for John Does, a week later.

Somehow this lady did not let it go and hounded the police until she found someone who could help her identify him. They exhumed his body and she was able to give him a proper funeral, which I attended.

Fast forward nine years to when I was about six months into my new career as a spiritualist. Daisy and I had decided to go for a drink at TGI Friday's. I looked across the bar and saw Andrew's smile on a man, and then the smile turned into Andrew's face. I burst into tears. I was not prepared for that. I hadn't thought of him in years. The wave of grief was so strong it overwhelmed me and I couldn't contain it.

I looked at Daisy and said, "Pay the check, I gotta go." And I ran out of the bar and into my car.

> What you are surrounded by, you will become, or it will become you.

Sitting there in the parking lot of the TGI Friday's, I cried for a few moments and then began to pray for Andrew. What was the purpose of all of this? Archangel Michael answered.

He showed me a picture of Andrew's earthbound spirit wondering around the neighborhood where he'd lived. He explained that Andrew needed my connection in order to ascend. He would have to remember that entire life and not just the trauma he'd experienced. That's why he called me to him in his final moments, so that I could help secure a safe passage back home for him when he was ready.

I called out to Andrew's spirit, *"I love you. Are you ready to go home?"*

I saw his face and his smile as he nodded at me.

"Do you see St. Michael?" I asked him.

His spirit then became light and he ascended with St. Michael. I wailed the entire thirty-minute ride home. I arrived back at the apartment much calmer. I was still in a little disbelief about the miracle I'd just witnessed. I also realized that I'd never really grieved Andrew's death. Being a witness at that time for a purpose had superseded the importance of grieving, but now that it was done, I'd have to truly mourn his loss.

The Slayer's Pact: Think for Yourself

The more you are aware of your spiritual world, the more it becomes imperative to know and understand yourself. Opening to the spiritual world means that you open up to all that you are connected to in a very intimate way, and it changes the way you relate to others on every level. Just as an empathic person must check with herself every time a new feeling strolls through to see if it belongs to her or another, we experience the same thing with our thoughts and ideas as well. What you are surrounded by, you will become, or it will become you: that's why it is imperative to have an understanding of yourself in order to remain independent. We often take on the feelings, thoughts, ideologies, and beliefs of those we surround ourselves by if we are not aware. So make sure you always get all the facts.

Ignorance is a man's best friend

First of all, let me give you my definition of ignorance. It is not the absence of information or truth; it is the setting aside of that information or truth in order to put the focus on the information that best serves the individual in his temporary and limited need, understanding, or agenda.

It is true that a person can only see as far as his needs will allow. For instance, humanity hasn't yet needed to unite as one in the presence of extraterrestrial visitation, so patriotism for one's nation has mostly been the dominant concern for humanity as a whole.

However, as we become more interconnected, we are definitely living in a time of less patriotism and more humanism. Just wait until we have a galactic event; then it will be easier for people to accept the human race and our interconnectedness as human beings, no matter our patriotic pursuits. That, however, is a topic for another book. I thought I would take this opportunity to focus on understanding the benefit that a mass emotional sentiment on a spiritual level would have on us.

> THE PROCESS OF THINKING, THE KAHUNAS BELIEVED, CREATES THOUGHT FORMS. AND, AS MOST THOUGHTS COME IN A TRAIN AND IN RELATION TO OTHER THOUGHTS, THE SHADOWY BODIES OF THOUGHTS (THOUGHT FORMS) GROUP IN CLUSTERS.
>
> BRAD STEIGER, KAHUNA MAGIC

Mass energetic support of an idea will change the outcome

When a bunch of people feel the same way about something, one of two things happen: what they feel either creates an energetic support for the universal truth or it is at odds with it.

A universal truth includes everyone. A lot of folks think that mass thinking, or the energy that is created from it, is dangerous, but in fact over time, mass thinking forces the universal truth to come out. Eventually, mass thinking will help those with exclusive thinking to assimilate and adopt a change of ideas that includes everyone. Mass thinking feels so dangerous because until the universal truth is integrated there often is great conflict. In the case of terrorism—an extremely and violently dangerous form of myopic perception—a terrorist's position that he will change mass sentiment with intimidation will ultimately become his enemy.

As the global community decides to align with the universal truth of interconnectedness, smaller communities will be able to integrate the strength that comes energetically from the global masses. The desire for terrorism will put the terrorists in conflict with themselves because their sentiment will not be in alignment with universal truth. The reality is that we are not separate from one another or separate from the Creator. The terrorists' conflicts will continue until there is a change in the balance of power, a change that is inevitable.

Ignoramuses are moved easily

The interesting thing about single-minded, ignorant people is that they are incredibly vulnerable on energetic and spiritual levels. I think that many folks respond to the nature of a terrorist's message by seeing the message as little more than juvenile. The terrorists kidnap and attack out of their belief in the importance and power of their righteous emotions, manhood, or belief systems disguised as spirituality and religion. Our true power and connection to the universe comes from the heart, not the emotional center or genitals. When you attack the terrorists' ideas you attack their manhood, whether they know it or not.

There are millions of people in alignment with each other questioning the terrorists' thoughts, motives, and means. Energetically or emotionally, when you directly oppose a person's idea of himself or a group's idea of itself, it naturally puts the person or group on the defense and in conflict with themselves. The person or group moves from an immature position of comfort and ideological stability, to a holistic position of connection with the universal truth. Whether consciously or subliminally, the terrorist recognizes whether his position is in alignment with the whole, and if not the terrorist (consciously or not) will be weakened and open to awakening. It is in that transition and new position that the terrorists are vulnerable to change.

The Slayer's Pact: **Think for Yourself**

Refuse to be terrorized: No terrorism

Don't get me wrong. If you have ever been victimized in any way, then you know what a beast it is to overcome the illusion of someone's power over you. At every moment before you overcome that illusion, they do, in fact, have power over you. But when you recognize that you give your authority to others or that you don't give your authority to others, you experience the most amazing feeling of personal power and internal freedom. It is in that moment that you truly align with the power of the great and let go of the fragility of the small.

Just so there are no misunderstandings, I am speaking purely of a concept that is truthful spiritually. I am not saying that if you have been victimized it is in any way your fault. What I *am* saying is that you have power whether you know it, feel it, or believe it. Your power actually goes all the way to superhero status. I believe it can take lifetimes of experience for a soul to learn to stand up in faith and in the face of punishing odds, to learn how truly to be powerful and how not to separate itself from others. It may take lifetimes, but that learning is inevitable.

> In other words delusional people, and people who separate themselves from others, align with the weakness of the narrow instead of with the power of the universal. They will inevitably be assimilated.

When you have been abused

I work with many people who have experienced abuse in some way in their lives, whether it is physical, sexual, or emotional abuse. The statistics are outrageous: as many as one in three women and one in five men will experience abuse in their lifetime. Twenty years ago it was commonly considered that if you'd been abused in some way, the best you could hope for in your life was to be able to manage the trauma and the triggers, but healing completely was not an option on the table. Today, complete healing is the only option and inevitable. Understanding the seven elements of spiritual process, helps you begin to understand that the Universe works in a specific way.

It is the same for everyone no matter who you are, where you come from, how hard you are willing to work, or whatever kind of education you have. We are all truly equal in this way. It can take lifetimes of spiritual incarnations to complete a dynamic, and we will spend our lives completing events and the residual effects of those events. Even if you don't really believe in past lives or prescribe to this philosophy, you have some sort of connection to the ideas presented here, indicating their value to you. Otherwise you wouldn't be reading this. People who truly have no need for this information, don't receive it.

Completing the event

To complete an event is a momentous occasion. It changes you on every level that you exist. A child who has been molested from early childhood will begin his process of change for that event the minute the event occurs. Ignorance in this case could manifest in the form of the child being too fearful to tell anyone what happened or even pretending that it did not happen.

Everything changes once the news is out. Resistance can manifest for this child as acting out, power struggles, extreme emotion, depression, and extreme behavior either aggressive or passive-aggressive. Conflict can manifest in the child slowly, over time, based on the circumstances. The child will experience and process the conflict physically, emotionally, mentally, and spiritually; and resistance will always end in a breakthrough that at the beginning is the acknowledgement of the event itself.

Surrender, then, is the beginning of the acceptance of the healing process. For the child, who could now be much older, this oftentimes results in facing the abuse and perpetrator in some way, and giving himself permission to find forgiveness for himself and the abuser.

Choice, for this child, means actually allowing feelings of powerlessness to be processed through grief, beginning to recognize where he is not feeling empowered in his life, and drawing his power back to his choices. Comedy for the child, now possibly a man, has a greater chance of happening the more he processes his grief.

The more comedy, the more he will relax and release the need to be hyper-vigilant in all aspects of his life. This is the time for far-reaching behavioral changes very different from the ones cultivated because of the abuse. These new behaviors begin the process of helping him to cultivate trust in himself and for others. Completion, for this man, comes from feeling vindicated in some way, and then finding total forgiveness for all people connected to the event.

> THOSE WHO CANNOT REMEMBER THE PAST ARE CONDEMNED TO REPEAT IT.
>
> GEORGE SANTAYANA

Completing the dynamic

Addiction is a powerful dynamic that everyone in some way will experience. Addiction is a way of relating to something. It is not the substance or object of the desire that we ultimately are addicted to. It is the behavior and belief that we apply to anything that is the addiction. The addict lies to himself and therefore to others. The dynamic to be completed, then, is the denial of the self.

Ultimately, this dynamic is completed when you recognize that there is no separation between man and God, that they are two vibrational perspectives of the same thing. What if you don't believe in God? This is why it can take lifetimes to complete a dynamic. There are important things you can learn about yourself by denying the existence of God, as well as important things you can learn by accepting the existence of God.

Accepting the existence of a Creator ultimately results in the discovery that separation between you and the Creator is an illusion, an illusion that nonetheless helps us better understand the nature of all things. It can take experiencing many philosophies, belief systems, and religions before one soul can comprehend on all levels the nature of the universe.

The end of a phase of spiritual process always leads to the beginning of another. The process of detachment from one idea always leads to the attachment to another, more expansive, idea. As you might have deduced by now, one process of spiritual change runs concurrently with many other processes of spiritual change and is never ending. We live in a multidimensional world with infinite possibilities, and we as human beings are made in the same image as the Creator, oneness.

What happens when you die

I was trying to explain to a fifteen-year-old about what happened to her mom when she died. It is a slightly unique situation, but getting more and more common every day.

Cara was so sad about her mother, and I knew her mother had been visiting her frequently in spirit. She'd been desperately trying to communicate for months now, and she didn't understand that her grief was keeping her from the awareness of her mom's presence. Cara may have received these visitations as a dream or longing for her mother. I knew that telling her the truth about what was happening with her mother right now would help eventually, but it might sting and ping with pain at the beginning.

Cara, although young in years, is a grown-up. She is wise beyond her years. Her adolescence was cut short with the abrupt and unexpected death of her mother from a drug-induced heart attack. I could feel from her behavior and sleep patterns that she was being visited at night and occasionally during the day. Mom was a little bitter at the moment for she still had not been able to accept her own loss. She could have never conceived that doing the drugs she thought were just for fun—you know, a casual habit—could weaken her to the point that her heart would give way. Unfortunately, what she wasn't aware of in herself was her grief, her life of unexpressed grief, the pain that she had been trying to cover up so valiantly with every drug she took.

I didn't know the lady, nor have I researched her spirit to know if her pain was from this life or the past, but I suspect she did not know either. Cara was one of three bright children with an incredibly diligent and loving father who'd taken care of the three children since his divorce from their mother. The mother's death came a bit of time later.

Cara began sitting and then pacing around the living room with a look on her face that was not her own; that's how I knew Mom was present.

"Hi, how are you doing?" I said.

"Uh, fine," she replied, as she paced.

Ah, teenagers, man. It's a rough time anyway, but wow. I thought. So I decided to just go for it. Break the ice to the subject I knew needed to be dealt with.

"So, you've been thinking about your mom a lot lately, huh?" I asked.

"How'd you know?" she snapped.

Her eyes brightened a bit and her heart slowed. Often, with an earthbound spirit, they begin to recognize when someone around them can see and understand them, and her mother had clearly gotten there.

Cara did not know that her mother was haunting her and that some of her actions, thoughts, and words were not really her own. With her newfound hormones, things were quite a struggle anyway. All her feelings that had risen to the surface were all so intense that she really could not discern the presence of her mother's energy compared to hers; but they were oh so different.

I said to Cara, "Tell me what you've been thinking about your mom."

"I really don't want to talk about it," she responded.

"I understand that you don't, but I feel really strongly that there are a few things that you need to know. Things that when you hear them might make you sad, but then relieved. These things might be able to put some experiences you're having in perspective for you, and maybe make a lot of sense."

"Why do you think that?" she asked.

"Well, let me ask you this: do you ever feel sad and angry for reasons that don't make any sense?"

"Yes."

"Do you ever find yourself getting really mad at your father, but then really sad about him as if you are a burden to him?"

Cara immediately burst into tears and ran from the room, screaming at me.

"How do you know?"

I gave it about five minutes and then walked into the kitchen where she was standing.

I asked, "Are you okay?"

As she sobbed quietly, she whispered, "How do you know these things."

"Come on."

I led her back to the living room. I got her a tissue that almost seemed to come out of nowhere, Dr. Phil style. She sat on the couch and I sat on the chair.

I said, "I feel like I should sit you on my lap to tell you all this."

And her eyes now caught mine, and we laughed. She was way too old, and her 5'11" frame definitely dwarfed me. Finally, Cara was there in full. Mom, however, was still in the room.

"Do you think that you are ready to know what I have to tell you?"

I know it doesn't seem rational, but the spirit isn't rational; it is creative. And you know how sometimes you just know if it's right or wrong at a particular moment. I was asking her to be intuitive about herself.

"Yes," she replied, with great confidence, "I think I am ready."

"Do you know what happens when people die?"

"They go to heaven," she replied.

"Well, eventually, but it's a little more complex than that. Everybody's situation is a little different and it depends on how they were doing and their level of awareness when they died."

"Oh, you mean if they are Christian or not? If they didn't have Jesus in their heart they don't go to heaven?"

"Well, that is one way to describe it, but let's talk about what all that means. Sometimes, when people die, they aren't expecting it. They don't believe that it can happen, maybe they aren't really paying attention to the needs of their physical body, or maybe they end up in a tragic accident, or are victimized in some way. Those people, oftentimes, need some extra time to understand and cultivate, what you call, their relationship with Christ, which is a way of being; it is an energy that we cultivate through learning and following the universal truths. God promises that we will live eternally with him and so people who die before really cultivating a consciousness of him, well, they continue to live without a body, until they get the information that they need in order to move on to the next life."

"Is that what happened with my mom?"

"I think so. I think that your mom did not understand that she could die, and it came unexpectedly for her. I also think that she was very sad about some things, and that when her body died her spirit was faced with all that sadness in its rawest form. You see, her body and her habits had been a buffer.

"Sometimes people take drugs and alcohol because they think that it helps them not to feel pain. It doesn't quite do that. It displaces the pain for a period of time. But if you don't feel what is yours, then whatever you don't feel is stored in your spirit until you are ready, and some people aren't ready and cannot learn things in a body that they can learn in spirit."

"Wow, I didn't know that."

"It kind of makes sense that you didn't because in our culture, we don't really teach that directly to people. We leave it up to religion and not everyone follows one religion. Different religions have different philosophies, yet they are all God's children just the same."

"Why don't some people have religion?"

"Because many of the religions out there exclude certain people and lack understanding. Well, I should say that the religion doesn't lack understanding, but that to receive understanding is the purpose of religion, and understanding cultivates a person's relationship with God. There are a lot of teachers out there who specialize in this, but sometimes religious people feel like these teachers are against God rather than just trying to teach about God, and well, sometimes people can be fearful and complicated. See what I mean about complex? We started talking about dying and it turned into a discussion about religion."

"Yeah," she said with a little sigh.

"There is one other thing that I think that you should know."

"Okay."

"When a spirit is left without a buffer for all of their feelings and information about themselves, when they are left without a body, sometimes they hang around to finish what they started. Every soul comes into this life with a goal of learning. Sometimes it's about feeling, sometimes it is about trust, but there is always a goal. The souls who are our family, well, they agree to it beforehand. So, you and your brother and sister, mom and dad, all agreed to be family. Sometimes we have obligations to that family that are left unfulfilled in a body. Do you understand what I mean?"

"No."

"I know, me either. That even sounded complicated to me. Let me try again. When your mom died she wasn't finished with her relationship to any of you kids, but I think especially with you. When she died she didn't understand the impact of her actions and how it would affect all of you, and other people in her life. She did not even know how she felt about a lot of things, until her body was gone and she had nothing else to do but sit with all of her thoughts, feelings, and beliefs. Right now she is sitting with the burden of her past pains and with the impact of her choices on other people, including you. Does that make more sense?"

"A little."

"Okay, well, that's progress."

We both laughed.

"Cara, I need for you to know...well, your mom needs for you to know, that she visits you often, and sometimes the thoughts that you have are her way of trying to communicate to you. She wants you to know how sorry she is, about everything. Right now, she is overwhelmed with how sorry she is, and how angry she is that she can't change things. Well, that she cannot be with you how she intended. Does that make any sense?"

After some time, Cara responded, "Sometimes I think of her and get so mad, and then I get sad and my stomach and heart hurt. I don't know why."

"It could be that when you feel those things that she is visiting you, and perhaps those are her feelings, and not yours."

Cara burst into tears and asked, "Is she here right now?"

"Yes, she is."

"My heart hurts so badly," said Cara.

Now we just sat there in silence. The room was full.

"Cara, take a deep breath, and take my hand. These feelings that you are having are not yours, they are your mother's. Take another deep breath. You are safe, and so is your mother. You do not have to take on her feelings, but I need for you to think about what she wants you to know, through her feelings."

"I think that she wants me to know that she is sad that she left me."

"Yes, that's good, Cara."

"I think that she is really confused, and now my head hurts."

"It's okay, Cara. Take another deep breath and remember that your body is your own. Cara, do you know the Lord's Prayer?"

"Yes," she replied.

"Let's say that together."

> *Our Father, who art in heaven,*
> *Hallowed be thy Name,*
> *Thy Kingdom come,*
> *Thy will be done on earth,*
> *As it is in heaven.*
> *Give us this day our daily bread.*
> *And forgive us our trespasses,*
> *As we forgive them that trespass against us.*
> *And lead us not into temptation,*
> *But deliver us from evil.*
> *For thine is the kingdom, the power, and the glory, forever and ever.*
> *Amen.*

"Mother, Father, God. Thank you for this glorious opportunity for mother and daughter to come together again in the light of your love. Lord, we ask that you soothe Cara's mother and the pain from which she suffers. Lord we ask that you give her your understanding and wisdom at this time so that her burden may be lifted. Lord, we ask today for you to show the entire family how to forgive themselves and each other for all that they did and did not do, for all that was right and wrong in their relationships to each other and to you, knowing that the compassion that is yours for them, will now fill their hearts for themselves and each other. And Lord, help them to grieve their pain deliberately, clearly, and in grace that with every storm of emotion comes a beautiful peace and knowing of your presence every day in their lives. And so it is. In your beautiful Son's name we pray. Amen"

Then we just sat there in silence. The room was full. I mean there were ancestors from both lineages there. And the angels packed the room—definitely a full house on that day.

> If you don't know love, you can't know true will power. True will is created through the unifying force of love.

How I Met John and Adele Battle

The only place to start this story is from the very beginning, to confess at least a few of the memories that I have of growing up with the vision, presence, and heart of John and Adele inside of me. This story, out of all of them, has been the hardest to tell. There is an intense fear that comes when you are to be revealed to others in a real way.

The voice in my head says, *Maybe they'll flat out think you're crazy*. But I suspect if that's the case, that ship has already sailed. Everyone who knows me, already knows.

Some, in their ignorance, have said things like, "Well, you are pro-black," or, "You know, 'they' do respond differently to her."

It is true, that many times in my life, white racists will look at me and speak freely as if beliefs come automatically with the color of your skin. When I was young, my face would turn red from anger, and I would think, "Don't they see who I am?"

I was working a sales job one time when a couple of kids, a beautiful dark-skinned boy and a lovely, very pale-skinned blonde girl around the age of sixteen, walked past. They were so beautiful and holding hands, looking delightfully in love. From their energy, they seemed well suited for each other.

That was the first thing I noticed until the white lady standing next to me said, "Oh, that poor girl is ruining her life."

My jaw dropped as I choked in some air. I took a beat to gather myself and then asked her, "What year is it?"

She looked at me strangely, and replied, "1993."

"You're a little behind the times, don't you think?" I said.

She jawboned a little at the confusion of being called out and then blurted, "Oh no, I'm not a racist. I'm married to a Mexican."

It is a very specific experience to carry the spirit of another. Growing up, I certainly didn't have this level of clarity in communication, but that seemed the least important to me. I had many spirits with me; they were my entourage, my people. As a child I experienced their presence through my empathy. Always, I saw through their eyes first. In fact, their eyes were my eyes, for as long as I can remember. Luckily, I had access to their wisdom and self-control as well.

Once when I was about five years old Grandma came to visit. It was Christmas time and we were all watching television in the family room. Grandma asked me to pass her the *nigger toes*. Immediately my eyes welled up with tears. I was confused and looked to my mother.

"Here, she wants the Brazil nuts," she explained.

I picked up the bowl of shelled nuts on the table and brought them to her. I laid back down on the floor and tried to hide my tears. I'd never heard that word before, but somehow I knew and felt its meaning. In truth, I probably only saw Grandma about ten or fifteen times in my life—she lived far away. And, I never once heard my parents speak in a racist manner about anyone. But my people knew, and gave me the truthful feelings that come with the damage of racism and bigotry, the feelings that propelled my voice and need, or rather the feelings that propelled my inability to accept subtle and common bigoted views from others, today.

As I got older, my experience became more encompassing through nighttime dreams and daytime visions. All through my childhood and on through high school, I would have this reoccurring dream of hundreds of burlap sacks of apples. I would wake up and see them stacked around my bed. The vision was visceral and made me break into a sweat every time. They were terrifying and made no sense at all. How could burlap sacks of apples be terrifying? Up until this point it was the spirit of John and his vision and voice that I perceived the strongest. Of course, Adele was there too, but her subtle strength and faith were usually overshadowed by the fear and anxiety that the impending memory of her demise perpetuated. I lived with it most of the time at that point in my life.

When I got to New York everything changed dramatically: my life, my environment, and my health. I moved to Harlem in 1985 on a burnt-out block, to my third-floor walk-up apartment, in a 1850s building that I squatted. My first real home. For the first time in my life I felt at peace and at home in an environment. Don't get me wrong. It was dangerous, but I suppose the level of danger suited my level of anger, so it was a win-win.

It was a building on which the previous owner owed so much in tax that the city took it. It just sat there for years falling apart. I came across a woman who was renting this apartment, and by *renting*, I mean she was sponsoring a squat-in. I didn't exactly understand whether or not we were breaking the law, but what I did know was that at the end of it, I would have a three-bedroom, rent-controlled apartment for two hundred dollars a month in New York City.

According to Marylin, a drug dealer from the neighborhood had been trying to move in and squat the building, but before he could complete renovations he was sent to jail, and she needed to get other people in there as soon as possible. So, when I moved in, the place had no windows— many holes for windows, but no actual windows. There was no lock on the door, only a padlock and chain to keep it closed. Obviously, as it was still winter it was too cold to stay there often, but I did on occasion, locking the padlock and chain on the inside during the night.

To supplement, I still had my room at the College Residence Hall, which was—for the most part—a single-room occupancy that was moderately well-kept, clean, and safe, up the hill on Broadway. For almost a year, it became a little battle between us and the city. They'd come out and cut off the chain and lock to the apartment and exchange it with a new one, and then Marylin and I would creep over in the middle of the night and cut it off and put another. As it turned out, a portion of the money we'd given to Marylin to finish renovations was actually given to an attorney. There was a group of about five of us that had put up funds and been instructed to send in rent checks to the City of New York, which unwittingly cashed them, not looking to see if there were actual leases attached. Once the checks had been cashed, the law declared that the city must give us all leases for the apartments in question.

No, their looks and compassion could have been simply due to a young lady left alone by her date, and they wanted for me to feel comfortable.

The first time I "saw" Adele, I was in a little bar on 127th Street and St. Nicholas in Harlem. It was the middle of the day, and I'd gone with a friend who was called away for a conversation just after we'd ordered a beer. There were two women chatting to the left of me and two men to the right, a single woman just on the other side of the men and a lovely woman my mother's age tending bar. Certainly everyone had taken notice of me. Was it that I was the only white person in the bar or—as I suspected—my combat boots, miniskirt, jean jacket with a fake fur collar with stuffed bear paws on each end and the fact that I looked like I was still in high school in a bar in the middle of the day.

No, their looks and compassion could have been simply due to a young lady left alone by her date, and they wanted for me to feel comfortable. From the moment my friend left, each person at the bar gave me a nod hello and let me listen in on their conversations while taking turns buying me beers.

The two men were having a discussion. Tiny, who was a gentleman in his fifties and stood about 6'7", was wearing a pair of high-water overalls that draped over his big round middle, with a straw hat and work boots. And Rico, who was also in his mid-age, wore a Members Only jacket with a pair of jeans and stood about 4'6". They were laughing because, evidently, Rico had his own personal mugger. Tiny was ribbing him because on the last three paydays, after cashing his check, a man waited for Rico outside the bar he always went to after work, stole his money, and then walked him home. You know, to make sure he got home safe. I laughed so hard, I cried.

This brought my attention to the bartender. She was a lovely, conservative lady who looked exactly like my mother (in this life), only with very dark skin. She was wearing a classic A-line skirted dress with a fitted bodice and a little fabric belt around the waist. Her hair was short in glossy black curls shaped nicely around her face. Her nose, cheek bones, and lips looked similar to my mom's. That got my attention.

But as I gazed at her, watching her chat with the other patrons, I became aware of Adele's quiet spirit of nonnegotiable faith, and my eyes welled up with tears. For just a brief moment I saw Adele's image standing in front of me as if it were a hologram, and then she was gone. As my awareness came back into the room, the bartender was serving me a beer that the ladies sitting to my left had bought. I lifted it in gratitude as we caught eyes.

Several times throughout those years in New York, I had experiences witnessing and experiencing racism and bigotry, subtle and overt. The hatred and ignorance that people carry with them is profound. Looking through my particular lens of compassion, the thing that stood out the most is that every person that was hateful to me, was worse to themselves. And I've been physically and emotionally abused, lied to, stolen from, and betrayed in many ways.

Every time something happened, a little voice in my head would say, *Amateurs*. And it always made me laugh. Everything that happened to me, I understood my connection to. While I didn't always feel empowered in every situation, my spirit said I could be if I tried. Nothing that anyone could have done to me was worse than what the spirits I carried with me had experienced, or was worse than what was contained within the soul memories that were my own. The people who were hateful to me were in pain and carried damage to their spirits, damage they had no idea how to heal or no idea that it could be healed.

What came next was the line in the sand. Through a series of events in that final year in New York, I had a choice to make: to live by love or hate. And hate was kicking my ass. I had carried the anger, anguish, and bitterness long enough. There truly was only one way to go, so I chose love. Soon I packed up the car and headed to Los Angeles to embark on the hardest ten years of my life: the excavation of my soul memories and the retrieval of the pieces of my spirit that were left damaged and unprocessed in other dimensions of the past.

Some friends of mine—Hope and her boyfriend Paul—were having a house guest one weekend, Paul's cousin Eric. They asked if I would join them for dinner and dancing, and off we went. Eric was a nice guy and we both found ourselves being quite comfortable. We had a sort of subtle kinship for some reason, almost as if we were siblings.

Towards the end of the night, Paul was really drinking heavily and wanted to stop for one more round. Hope had taken the car keys and didn't mind, so we popped into a little spot in West Hollywood. Hope and I were walking back from the bathroom when I saw Paul who stood a good six to eight inches over Eric, holding two shots of whiskey and shouting as loud as he could for Eric to drink one. The rage in Paul's face and the fear in Eric's really struck me.

What could possibly be going on over there?

I thought that maybe as we came closer to where they were standing that Paul would notice and stop whatever shenanigan he was going through, but he didn't. It only escalated and he became more shockingly vile, while Eric was literally paralyzed in fear. Paul in this reality was black, but when I looked at him from afar, I saw the imprint of a white man filled with rage.

Hmmm, who is that? This is absolutely ridiculous, I thought as I came back to this time and space.

I walked over and stood in front of Eric and firmly said, "I don't know what this is about, Paul, but you need to stop it right now. Eric does not want to drink the whiskey, so he's not going to drink the whiskey. We are leaving now."

Something about my interruption of the circumstance stopped Paul's train of thought, and he looked at me like he was confused. Then he snickered, and we all headed for the door. We continued on to breakfast, but the dynamic between Paul and Eric got worse. Next thing I knew, Paul and Hope left, leaving me with Eric and without a ride.

> Through a series of events in that final year in New York, I had a choice to make: to live by love or hate.

Eric and I sat at that little diner for at least another hour talking, hoping Paul would answer his phone or come back to deal with the situation, but he didn't. Eric was left stranded without a place to go. Fortunately, I felt completely at peace around him, so I offered him my couch.

The next four days were really interesting. Neither Paul nor Hope ever called, and Eric and I really enjoyed each other's company. He helped me with things around the house; we cooked and talked about life and our experiences. We had a subtle emotional bond, again, like family.

On the fourth day around one o'clock in the afternoon, Paul called. He was outside in the car, and if Eric wanted a ride back to Texas, he had to leave now. Within ten minutes, he was out the door, and as it shut I fell to my knees. The reality I was living in disappeared, and my world became dark for a minute.

I saw Adele, being dragged by her hair, out the door by a couple of white boys. A noose was placed around her neck, and before I could take another breath she was strung up and her spirit was leaving her body. I felt *my* spirit leave *my* body and I knew that it was me. I had been Adele in that life. That was me and I was dead with no warning, no time, no control, no power—just dead. I wailed on the floor for at least another hour, crying almost nonstop for the next seven days.

As I processed her death and my healing, I finally understood that John had been with me the whole time, too. I understood, because as I grieved and forgave the men who had murdered me, I was able to find forgiveness for myself. And with that forgiveness came the spiritual understanding and wisdom I needed to let them go and let the spirits of John and Adele Battle finally rest.

For the first time in this life, they were gone from me, and I was left just a white girl. It literally wasn't until that moment that I understood what others assumed of me because of my race. I'd never seen it, felt it, or experienced it—until that moment.

Hmmm, I thought, *good to know.*

The Slayer's Ritual: Finding Your Transpersonal Cultural Beliefs

The pain of the damage caused by cultural, national, or religious belief systems is profound and healing the deeply held scars of your ancestors is a gift like no other. It is not time that heals all wounds, but metabolizes the many layers of pain and anguish that a limited belief can bring, over time, to the believer and to the ones impacted by the beliefs. At some point in your evolution, the beliefs that once protected you become your own personal nemesis and harbinger of strife. It is human to need pain in order to incite change, but that state is not permanent.

Finding your voice and the words to communicate it through compassion is the ultimate result. Speaking your mind and heart in a way that requires reception yet does not perpetuate ignorance and hate is the eventual end to your evolution and the beginning of your freedom. When this occurs, you no longer are fearful of the possibility of another's power over you and your life, environment, and circumstances. In this moment and place you understand and embrace the Universe that you create for yourself, finding love in all of it. You have fully moved through, courage, bravery, and pride into dignity, integrity, and fullness. In this new house of beliefs, there are only the limitations of your dreams and your imagination.

Know that as you heal yourself, you allow your ancestors to be released of their bondage as well. Take a few moments to write down on a piece of paper any thoughts and feelings you have about others regarding;

- race
- religion
- country
- music
- physical appearance
- gender
- sexual identity
- politics

Take as much time and space as you need for each topic, having patience for and acceptance with anything that you may find yourself writing about. This is the time to let all of your personal scary monsters out of the closet. Don't judge what you write, just write, write, write. This ritual you can implement over eight days, writing on one topic a day until finished. When harsh or uncomfortable feelings come up allow them expression and then allow them to move on. Once you are finished with the writing, take two days' rest. On the eleventh day, read all you have written and say goodbye. Burn all of your writing work with this prayer or one of your own creation in a burning pot or fireplace.

Creator, I now know there is no separation between all of your children and you, that we are all eternally linked. I forgive myself and all others for my judgments of myself and the judgments I put upon my loves, family, and global neighbors. Show me the way to your heart, Creator, and teach me of the dignity, integrity, fullness that is my birthright. I love you as I love myself as I love all others. I embrace this on all levels, in your glory.

The Slayer's Altar: Transpersonal Integration

What you'll need:

- A white, yellow, gold candle
- A bowl of corn or cornmeal
- 3x5 index card that says, *Thank you*

Affirmation: I am connected to all things as they are connected with me: It is safe to learn what I don't know about others.

Epilogue

The sacred essence of our lives connect across time. Linked by a primeval existence that reverberates at the very core of who we are, taking us on a journey of the ages. Now that we've walked with one another on the red road, I hope you see it fit to say, "I'm a little more at peace with change." That you recognize fear at your back door and not your front. And, that you embrace the human race, Mother Earth that sustains us all, the universe we all live in, and The Creator of whom we are all creations made of One Love.

Demon slaying is not just for warriors, as we are all warriors for love in our own way. Whether you are a watcher or a slayer; your presence, contribution, and affect on others and this planet is indisputable and invaluable. You have power beyond the limits of our current cultural understanding and are learning to embrace it at a very unique period of time with billions of other people in tow.

Science has now proven many things, first that our brain changes continually based on our thoughts and behaviors. Second, that emotions promoted by cultural beliefs have a defined and palpable impact on our physical health. And, third, that we are not relegated solely to the pattern or life condition that our DNA would suggest. With all of the new and profound information available it is not a stretch to embrace that we are impacted by the life and health of our planet or that it is impacted by ours. Or, that we see, feel, and hear the vibrations of a soul essence before our bodies send the signal to the brain to let the eyes know to see the body attached. It makes the existence of bigotry in any form, parochial. The implications of this truth on the hearts of many is life transforming. The opportunity to be personally responsible and accountable for all of the information that you communicate to others and the universe, long before you even speak or are visually seen; is penetrating.

The power that this truth endows is all yours to wield. Not just against something, but *for* something. The more you use your power towards the creation or transformation of what fills your heart, the more it brings peace to your mind and your world. Slaying your demons becomes simple with this understanding. The fight and struggle is not with the demon at hand it is with your fear that the demon promotes. No fear: no demon. All love.

Bibliography

Dale, Cyndi. *The Subtle Body: An Encyclopedia of Your Energetic Anatomy*. Boulder, CO: Sounds True, 2009.

Gerber, Richard. *Vibrational Medicine: The #1 Handbook of Subtle-energy Therapies*. 3rd ed. Rochester, VT: Bear & Company, 2001.

Gladwell, Malcolm. *The Tipping Point: How Little Things Can Make a Big Difference*. New York: Back Bay Books/Little, Brown and Company, 2002.

Glynn, Ian. *An Anatomy of Thought: The Origin and Machinery of the Mind*. Oxford: Oxford University Press, 1999.

Hanson, Rick. *Buddha's Brain: The Practical Neuroscience of Happiness, Love, and Wisdom*. Oakland, CA: New Harbinger Publications, 2009.

Hawkins, David R. *Power vs. Force: The Hidden Determination of Human Behavior*. Carlsbad, CA: Hay House, 2002.

Kornfield, Jack. *After the Ecstasy, the Laundry: How the Heart Grows Wise on the Spiritual Path*. New York: Bantam Books, 2000.

Lipton, Bruce. *The Biology of Belief: Unleashing the Power of Consciousness, Matter, and Miracles*. Santa Rosa, CA: Mountain of Love/Elite Books, 2005.

Lorler, Marie-Lu. *Shamanic Healing within the Medicine Wheel*. Translated by Matt Schulze and Winter Laite. Albuquerque, NM: Brotherhood of Life, 1991.

Martinez, Mario E. *The Mindbody Code: How to Change the Beliefs That Limit Your Health, Longevity, and Success*. Boulder, CO: Sounds True, 2014.

Paulson, Genevieve Lewis. *Kundalini and the Chakras: A Practical Guide—Evolution in this Lifetime*. St. Paul, MN: Llewellyn Publications, 1991.

Restak, Richard M. *The New Brain: How the Modern Age is Rewiring Your Mind*. Emmaus, PA: Rodale, 2003.

Steiger, Brad. *Kahuna Magic*. West Chester, PA: Whitford Press, 1982.

———. *Totems: The Transformative Power of Your Personal Animal Totem*. New York: HarperCollins Publications, 1997.

Wilson, James L. *Adrenal Fatigue: The 21st Century Stress Syndrome*. Petaluma, CA: Smart Publications, 2001.

Permissions

Some quotes required permission to be used in this text. Much effort was made in obtaining the permission of copyright holders of these quotes. I gratefully acknowledge permissions granted to quote from the following:

Alan Cohen, http://www.alancohen.com/. Used by permission of author.

Tracy Renee Jones, http://tracyrcncejones.com/. Used by permission of author.

Marie-Lu Lorler, *Shamanic Healing within the Medicine Wheel*, published by the Brotherhood of Life, 2002. Used by permission of publisher.

Mario Martinez, *The Mindbody Code: How to Change the Beliefs that Limit Your Health, Longevity, and Success*. Used by permission of author.

Stephen J. Miller, *The Keepers of Mana'an*. Used by permission of publisher.

Caroline Myss, "Daily Message Archive," http://www.myss.com/library/dailymessage/. Used by permission of author.

Brad Steiger, *Kahuna Magic*. Used by permission of author.

Brad Steiger, *Totems: The Tranformative Power of Your Personal Animal Totem*. Used by permission of author.

Other works by the author

CONQUER YOUR KARMIC RELATIONSHIPS: Heal Spiritual Trauma to Open Your Heart and Restore Your Soul, *(Volume Three, Demon Slayer's Handbook Series)*

In this ground breaking book, Dunblazier takes a look at your spiritual imprints and the repetitive patterns that position you in life. Understanding what karma is and learning all the ways to reveal, accept, forgive, and transform your relationships in every dimension. Not only to your soulmate beloveds and romantic entanglements, but how you relate to; food, money, family, culture, religion, sex, death, and your environment. This fascinating read will help you unearth the very core of what drives you, showing you how to direct its power into usable, life-giving resources for you and all your relations.

"This should be mandatory reading for anyone who wants to live a more peaceful and joyous life."—**Stephanie Chandler,** CEO of the Nonfiction Authors Association

MASTER YOUR INNER WORLD: Embrace Your Power with Joy *(Volume One, Demon Slayer's Handbook Series)*

Winner of the Coalition of Visionary Resources, Visionary Awards gold medal in Alternative Sciences and bronze medal in Shamanism, categories. Tracee covers many relevant topics such as: spirit guides and other dimensional entities, tools for healing, the spiritual purpose of anger, grief, and depression and how to transform strong emotions. You'll receive a new framework for healing from the soul to the body in a way that adjusts your perspective of the underworld and shows you the magnitude of your power in any situation. This book is a game changer for anyone who suffers.

"An encouraging playbook for would-be demon-slayers."—**Kirkus Reviews**

RAINBOW WARRIOR ACTIVATION DECK

Winner of the Living Now Gold medal, this brilliantly rendered and colorful 52 card deck set with a 124 page guidebook, created by national award-winning author and shaman—Tracee Dunblazier, and acclaimed intuitive artist—Justine Serebrin, is an inspiring solution for rising above the divergent forces all around us.

Whether you're using it for meditation—reading for pleasure or profession, it's exactly the tool you need.

This is the deck that grows with you.

"A knock-out of the park activation deck for use during meditation, as well as shadow and ascension work."—**Melinda Carver,** Author & Columnist

About the Author

Tracee Dunblazier GC-C, is a Los Angeles-based spiritual empath, shaman, and a six-time national award-winning author. As a multi-sensitive, Tracee's blend of intuitive information combined with different modalities, has provided the opportunity for thousands to achieve deep healing and create the success and peace they seek in their lives.

Empathic, delightfully vulnerable, and profoundly real—Dunblazier's two new keynotes: "Are You Haunted?" and "Conquer Your Karmic Relationships!" are enlightening presentations that will open your mind to what is happening right in front of you; the multiple energetic dimensions we all share. No matter where you sit on the spectrum of understanding, Tracee makes tangible the connection between mental wellness and spirituality. Many of us don't fully see what is holding us back from our dreams and aspirations—after these seminars; your eyes will be opened.

Tracee's compassionate, humorous, down-to-earth style empowers her clients, readers, and listeners to address difficult topics with courage and clarity. Because of this, Tracee is consistently called upon by the media for expert commentary on spirituality and relationship dynamics.

In 2015, she founded GoTracee Publishing LLC. It has since grown to be a nationally awarded hybrid-publisher that specializes in spiritual-healing and narrative non-fiction books, and divination oracle decks—tools for meditation and self-discovery. Their best-selling Demon Slayer's Handbook Series and Rainbow Warrior Activation Deck offer light in dark places. Game changers for those who suffer. GoTracee's publications expand the reader's understanding of spiritual transformation and offer the knowledge one needs to live their best life.

www.TraceeDunblazier.com

www.BeASlayer.com